# about eva

# all about eva

## A Holocaust-Related Memoir, with a Hollywood Twist

## by Vincent Brook

Foreword by Tom Tugend

gefen publishing house
JERUSALEM • NEW YORK Est. 1981

*To Bill Brandon, who devoted himself with great fervor*
*to the book's publication, helped make it the best it could be,*
*but sadly did not live to see it all the way through.*

Copyright © Vincent Brook
Jerusalem 2021/5781

Cover Design: Rita Lascaro
Typesetting: Rita Lascaro

ISBN: 978-965-7023-76-1
1 3 5 7 9 8 6 4 2
Library of Congress Control Number: 2021906284

Gefen Publishing House Ltd.        Gefen Books
6 Hatzvi Street        c/o Baker & Taylor Publisher Services
Jerusalem 9438614,        30 Amberwood Parkway
Israel        Ashland, Ohio 44805
972-2-538-0247        516-593-1234
orders@gefenpublishing.com        orders@gefenpublishing.com

**www.gefenpublishing.com**

Printed in Israel

# contents

Acknowledgments     vii

Foreword     ix

Prologue     3

Chapter 1     *Ninotchka*     7

Chapter 2     "King of the Eastern Jews"     13

Chapter 3     *Kristallnacht*     19

Chapter 4     Writing on the Wall     25

Chapter 5     A Taste of Honey     33

Chapter 6     Pandora's Box     37

Chapter 7     Bruch's List, Part 1     43

Chapter 8     Bruch's List, Part 2     49

Chapter 9     *Alles Geht Caputh* (Everything Goes "Kaput")     53

Chapter 10     Baggage Claim     61

Chapter 11     The Medium Is the Massage     65

Chapter 12     One-downsmanship     71

Chapter 13     Riffkele     75

Chapter 14     From Malka to Lemberg     77

Chapter 15     The New Weimar     81

Chapter 16     Trouble in Paradise     87

Chapter 17     Auld Lang Syne     91

Chapter 18     Rhapsody in Red     97

Chapter 19    Unholy Trinity                                    101

Chapter 20    Doubting Thomas                                   107

Chapter 21    "Pop Goes the Weasel"                             113

Epilogue                                                        119


Timelines & Appendices                                          125

Timelines                                                       127

Appendix A    Ernst Lubitsch and Billy Wilder                  130

Appendix B    Max Reinhardt and the Expressionist Movement     131

Appendix C    Helene Weigel and Elisabeth Bergner              133

Appendix D    Erwin Piscator and Bertolt Brecht               135

Appendix E    City Symphonies                                  136

Appendix F    G. W. Pabst and Louise Brooks                    137

Appendix G    *Haganah*                                         139

Appendix H    Persecution of Homosexuals in the Third Reich    141

Appendix I    Hollywood and Hitler                             142

Appendix J    Adolph Zukor and the Jews Who Invented
              Hollywood                                         143

Appendix K    Galician Jews                                     145

Appendix L    Varian Fry                                        146

Appendix M    Fritz Lang                                        148

Appendix N    Robert Ryan and Cornel Wilde                     149


Notes                                                           151

Index                                                           161

About the Author                                                171

# acknowledgments

Neither the author nor the subject matter of this memoir would exist without my parents, Rudy and Eva Brook. Besides bringing me into the world and living the extraordinary lives that inspired this true story, they bequeathed a treasure trove of written and oral documentation that bolsters its credibility and brings it to life. Rudy and Eva's close friends, and mine as well, Trudy Dresdner and Annchen Ikenberg (now deceased); my sadly departed cousin, Peter Meyer; his brother Tommi Meyer; and two close friends, Selma Benjamin and Lois Weinman, both very much alive at 100-years-young—all contributed valuable conversational and written information that affirmed and elaborated upon my parents' story. Other friends, Michael Odenheimer and Dana Dunlap, unearthed corroborating historical evidence; John McClintock helped investigate the location of my parents' sojourn in Sweden; Aubrey Pomerance of the Jewish Museum in Berlin provided access to the no-longer-in-print history of Gertrud Feiertag's Jewish school in Caputh; Tom Pfister helped obtain photos and, along with Frank Epstein especially, contributed to an important rethinking of the book's subtitle; and both Tom and Frank, along with countless others, aided my search for a new publisher after my original publisher Bill Brandon's passing. Jackie Gmach's connection to Gefen Publishing, however, proved the game-changer, leading me directly to owner/publisher Ilan Greenfield and a new lease on life for my memoir. Donna Rifkind's new book, *The Sun and Her Stars*, revealed a key detail about Alexander Granach's relationship with Salka Viertel. And though his role in the narrative is ambivalent at best, Alexander Granach's autobiography (Transaction Publishers), with an excellent introduction by Herbert Lewis, supplied invaluable backstory, as did the memoir (Atara Press) of his son, Gad Granach, now also deceased. The legion of archives, photo collections, and individuals whose help in acquiring images immeasurably enhanced the book include (listed alphabetically): Heinz Aalders of *De Parelduiker* magazine; Alamy Stock Photos; Chana Benjaminson of Chabad-Lubavitch; Jacob Engelhart; Adam Gershwin of the George Gershwin Trust; Elhad Harouvi of the Palmach Archive; Nancy Hartman of the United States Holocaust Memorial Museum; Benjamin Kuntz; Rosemarie Kutschis and Jens Tremmel of the Deutsches Literaturarchiv (DLA) Marbach; Petra Linnemann of Zorro Filmverleih; Michael Locke; Miriam Meyer; Michael Odenheimer; Michael Owen and Michael Stronsky of the Leonore and Ira Gershwin Trust; Photofest, Inc.; Hilde Recher of the Ölbaum Verlag; Chamisa Redmond and Paul Sommerfeld of the Library of Congress; Hans-Dieter Rutsch; David Sigler of the Oviat Library at California State University, Northridge; Sabine Solchow of the Akademie der Künste; Ruth Splansky; Britta Traub of the Norton Simon Museum; Michaela Ullmann and Louise Smith of the Lion and Marta Feuchtwanger collection at the University of Southern California (USC); Alisabeth Von Presley of Theatre Cedar Rapids; Kurt Wahlner; and Marc Wannamaker of Bison Archives. My cousin Timon Meyer and his assistant Eric Herbstreit in Berlin went the extra mile (or kilometer) as my liaison with European photo sources, and Matt "Where there's a will there's a way!" Gatlin did his usual yeoman's job of grabbing film frames. Michael Locke, besides providing original photos, also did much of the overall image scanning. The late Bill Brandon, publisher of Decalogue Books, which initially picked up the project, and independent readers Brian Gately, Jo Ann Gardner, and Kristen Donnan, greatly improved the book through their thoughtful editorial input, as did Rita Lascaro through her creative layout design. Special recognition and gratitude go out to Tom Tugend for his gracious Foreword. And as always, through the highs and lows, my wife, Karen, the love of my life, has been my anchor and inspiration, and the person who makes it all worthwhile.

# foreword

In his latest, most personal work, Vincent Brook draws on both his parental connections with various Hollywood luminaries and his own childhood on a chicken farm in the San Fernando Valley section of Los Angeles. But thematically, *All About Eva* is a double-header, whose most interesting theme is the assimilation to America of his parents, Rudy and Eva Brook, as refugees from Germany, during the time when Hitler's anti-Jewish decrees gradually but inexorably tightened the screws on the nation's Jewish inhabitants.

While Vincent's mother, Eva, is the pivotal character—whose suspected and real extra-marital relations, including an affair with a noted European actor, are described in considerable detail by the author—his steady and hard-working father, Rudy, is more typical of the highly educated refugees who started over from scratch on their arrival in America.

Rudy Bruch (before having anglicized the family name) was a young lawyer in Berlin, about to be named to a judgeship, when the roof fell in with Hitler's ascension to power. A veteran Zionist, Rudy prepared himself to become an agricultural worker in Palestine, while Eva's eyes were directed toward America. As became a pattern, Eva's preferences won out.

Not that the Brooks would have wished it, but the misfortunes of war in America, which included the internment of all immigrant Japanese and Japanese Americans on the West Coast, ended up working to Rudy Brook's advantage. The Japanese had held a practical monopoly on tending the impressive gardens of the movie stars and millionaires in Beverly Hills and Bel Air. That left Rudy, who benefited additionally from his and Eva's connections to the sizable European refugee community, as one of the few skilled non-Asian gardeners around. Rudy's high-end clientele, along with his tenacity and hard work, plus the sale of the chicken farm Vincent grew up on, eventually allowed the Brooks to build a house in the upscale community of Pacific Palisades with a stunning view of the ocean.

My own connection to the Brooks goes back to Germany, where my parents had befriended Rudy and Eva in better times in Berlin. I profited from this relationship when I enrolled in a rustic Jewish boarding school in Caputh, a Berlin suburb. Eva was my vigorous gym teacher at the school, while Rudy worked there as a part-time business manager. As Vincent describes, the school was intended as a haven from the Nazis, and indeed I have mainly fond memories of my time there, brightened by some of the most innovative and caring teachers I have ever known. They somehow created a sheltered island amid the approaching storm, with only a few incidents when the outside reality broke through. One such occurred on a hike through the nearby woods, when we were waylaid by a bunch of Hitler Youth who started cursing and spitting on us. Even this incident had a comparatively happy ending, however, when our adult leader, the school's physical education instructor, a burly Jew from Denmark, beat up the biggest of our tormentors, after which the rest beat a quick retreat.

After I also fortunately managed to emigrate to America and renewed contact with the Brooks, another fond memory is of a summer break in my college years, when Rudy hired me as an unskilled but willing assistant, and together we manicured the extensive Beverly Hills lawns of Ira Gershwin, the brother and lyricist of famed composer George Gershwin.

Rudy's and Eva's having rubbed shoulders with celebrities—Eva's literally as a masseuse—likely influenced Vincent's own interest in the entertainment industry. He went on to work as a film editor and screenwriter, and has spent the bulk of his career as a lecturer in media studies at major universities including the University of

Southern California (USC) and the University of California, Los Angeles (UCLA). The numerous books he has authored or edited also focus mainly on Hollywood and its extensive Jewish component. He has now applied his lively style and keen observations to a personal family saga. It's both a highly engrossing and entertaining read.

Tom Tugend, Los Angeles
January 2021

*Tom Tugend and his daughter, Alina*

TOM TUGEND is an award-winning journalist and a former science writer and communications director at UCLA. He is a contributing editor to the *Jewish Journal of Greater Los Angeles* and the Los Angeles correspondent for *The Jerusalem Post* (Israel), *The Jewish Chronicle* (London), and the global wire service of the Jewish Telegraphic Agency. He also has written extensively for the *Los Angeles Times* and *San Francisco Chronicle*. He is a veteran of World War II, Israel's War of Independence, and the Korean conflict, and has been inducted into the French Legion of Honor.

all about eva

*Anne Baxter in* All About Eve *(Photofest)*  *My mother, Eva Eger Bruch/Brook*

# prologue

The London stage adaptation of the movie *All About Eve* in 2019, and a proposed filming of the play in 2020, have thankfully rekindled awareness of the like-named Academy Award-winning Best Picture of 1950. Likely not enough, however, to compensate for the Oscar telecast's woeful ratings and the comparative indifference of even my college film students to what was once "Event TV," bigger than the Super Bowl and on a global scale. Thus, I feel some additional information is warranted about the kinship between that classic film and this part memoir/part historical novella.

More than just a punster's indulgence, *All About Eva* relates to its filmic namesake in several ways: first, in their nearly contemporaneous Hollywood movie and Broadway theater milieus. More significant is Anne Baxter's title role as one of filmdom's most notorious femmes fatales, with her character's given name (and my mother Eva's German equivalent) a nod to the ill-starred temptress from the Book of Genesis. Perceived by stage diva Margo Channing (played by Bette Davis) as a fawning fan and hired on as her factotum and protégée, Baxter's Eve Harrington winds up using her alleged idol as a stepping stone for her own rise to fame and eventually replaces Margo atop the Broadway heap—yet, at film's end, with another Eve waiting in the wings.

While my German-Jewish émigré mother didn't become or even aspire to be a star herself, she became, in her early thirties, a masseuse in Hollywood to several of them. The job was provided by a friend and fellow émigré who had established a massage salon catering to movie people in general and the burgeoning Los Angeles

*Alexander Granach (USC Feuchtwanger Collection )*

*Elisabeth Bergner (Alamy)*

influx of refugees from Nazi Germany in particular. Among the latter was famed Polish-Jewish actor Alexander Granach, whose surname, like Eva's married name Bruch, is pronounced with a rolling "r" and a raspy "ch"—and with whom she would have an adulterous affair. A renowned figure on stage and screen during the Weimar era (the period between the end of World War I in 1919 and Hitler's rise to power in 1933, named for the central German city where the country's short-lived postwar Constitution was written), Granach was relegated to supporting roles upon his fleeing to the United States in the late 1930s. His un-supporting role in my family's life in America adds a troubling note to the Hollywood twist of the book's subtitle.

Granach's womanizing also figures uncannily in this memoir's titular pun—and in a manner unforeseen by the author. Among the actor's many dalliances during the Weimar era was a torrid affair with Austrian-Jewish actress Elisabeth Bergner, who became a gardening client of my father's. Most remarkably, while performing on Broadway in 1943 (in the already suggestively titled *The Two Mrs. Carrolls*), she had an *All About Eve*-like experience, when a seemingly innocent young woman whom she'd hired as her secretary tried to "take over" Bergner's life. Upon learning of the incident from Bergner, American actress and author Mary Orr used it as the basis for a short story, *The Wisdom of Eve*, which appeared in *Cosmopolitan* magazine in 1946. The story was then adapted for the stage, and the play went on to inspire writer-director Joseph Mankiewicz's 1950 Academy Award-winning film. An added irony to Bergner's alleged victimization by an Eve-like temptress is that she herself was a notorious femme fatale who, according to Granach's son, Gad, "used her lovers as a springboard for her career," Granach prominently among them. Though not the main focus of this memoir, the Bergner subplot will be revisited at various points.

My German-Jewish émigré father, Rudy, meanwhile, as Tom Tugend glossed in the Foreword, would become a gardener to the stars, building his celebrity clientele on his wife Eva's refugee-colony connections. Both my parents had faced considerable hardships during the early Nazi period (Granach had fled already in 1933), and though they would lose a number of close relatives in the Holocaust (Granach was more fortunate in that regard), all three found refuge in America in 1938. And so it was that just as the Hollywood film industry

*My father, Rudy Bruch/Brook*

had been founded in the early 1900s largely by Jews who had fled an earlier round of virulent European anti-Semitism, my parents and Granach, due to Hitler's genocidal Jew-hatred, ended up in, and taking advantage of, the movie capital.

What follows, then, is a harrowing yet also uplifting saga—cobbled together, collage-like, from written documents, oral histories, published autobiographies, my own recollections, and imagined recreations—of a German-Jewish émigré couple and a Polish-Jewish interloper caught up in the tumult and frenzy of the first half of the twentieth century, both helped and haunted by Hollywood's glamour and grotesquerie.

The events are not presented chronologically. Rather, like the varied content sources, the timeline follows a zigzag pattern that I feel better captures the ups and downs of the years prior to and during World War I, the Weimar and Nazi periods, and World War II, that both Granach and my parents lived through. Even the United States, while providing a comparative safe haven and job opportunities, didn't prove a panacea for these and other German-Jewish immigrants. Like all Jews, foreign and domestic, they faced less lethal but still palpable anti-Semitism in America, as we'll see.

This real-life story, with some educated guesses to fill in the gaps, opens soon after my parents' and Granach's arrival in America, just as the aforementioned romantic triangle was taking shape and Eva's affair with Granach was starting to gel. The time is summer 1939, the place an MGM studios sound stage in Los Angeles, where the soon to be Oscar-nominated best picture *Ninotchka*, co-starring Greta Garbo and Melvyn Douglas (with Alexander Granach among the supporting cast), is shooting its final scene.

## CHAPTER 1

# *Ninotchka*

The onlooker's shy glance caused his eyes to dilate . . . in amorous anticipation. "There's gold in them thar hills," Granach thought, chuckling at the double entendre, and at the image of himself as Chaplin in *The Gold Rush* doing the famous dance of the dinner rolls, only with a pair of gefilte fish. "How young was Lita Grey—Charlie's latest on-screen and backstage lover—sixteen, seventeen? And the little devil got away with it, even with everyone thinking he was a Jew!"

"CUT!" yelled Ernst Lubitsch, though his German accent nudged the word closer to "cat." "Vat ze hell are you laughing at, Granach? Zat's Garbo's job!"

Cast and crew exploded at the reference to "Garbo laughs!"—the promotional hook for *Ninotchka*, the screwball comedy they were shooting. Besides a play on "Garbo talks!"—the pitch for her first sound film, *Anna Christie* (1930)—Garbo's laughter plays a major role in *Ninotchka*.

Garbo's eponymous grim Soviet agent parodied both the repression of Stalinist Russia and the Swedish beauty's famously melancholy persona. And both are hilariously upended midway through the film when—sitting stone-faced in a Paris bistro while her would-be lover, Count D'Algout (Melvyn Douglas), rattles off joke after corny joke in a vain attempt to crack her robotic shell—she finally breaks into uproarious laughter. But not from the jokes. The epiphany, the film's punchline, and one of the high points in Hollywood cinema comes only when the dapper D'Algout, increasingly frustrated by his inability to wring even a smile from the Commie martinet, falls

*Before and after "Garbo laughs" in* Ninotchka: *above: Greta Garbo and Melvyn Douglas; below: Felix Bressart, Garbo, Sig Ruman, and Alexander Granach (both Photofest)*

over backwards onto the floor—causing not only Ninotchka but the entire bistro's mainly working-class patrons to split their sides at the aristocrat's comeuppance. A Freudian slip with Marxist overtones—and straight from the belly of the beast!

"Vas I laughing?" stammered Granach, echoing Lubitsch's Teutonic tinge.

"Vell it sure vasn't *Hamlet!*"

More laughter rocked the set.

"But Ernst, seriously," Granach pleaded above the din, "ziss scene is ridiculous!"

"And *seriously* is how you should play it!" Lubitsch retorted.

Gritting his teeth, Granach held up the picket sign he was holding that read "Buljanoff Iranoff Unfair to Kopalski!" and turned to the near six-footer standing next to the gnomish Lubitsch.

"You wrote ziss sing, Billy! Can you tell me vy I am doing ze protesting?"

"Ass you are doing now?" Billy Wilder quipped in the third German accent in a row, causing even Lubitsch to join in the collective mirth.

But Granach had a point. This was *Ninotchka*'s final scene. Yet rather than have the curtain go down on co-stars Garbo and Douglas, whose climactic lovers' kiss in the penultimate scene would have both satisfied genre convention and signified Capitalist/Communist rapprochement—the film tacks on a non sequitur. As the shooting script described and theaters and Turner Classic Movies would later show, camera tilts down at night from a restaurant's neon sign—"Buljnaoff...Iranoff...Kopalski" (the last name un-illuminated)—to Granach on the sidewalk holding his placard. Yet other than the sign leaving only "Kopalski" in the dark, no grounds are given for his character's disapproval. Not only had the three Russian emissaries been on friendly terms throughout, but the penultimate scene saw them jointly celebrating their, and Ninotchka's, defection from the Soviet Union and her reunion with D'Algout. So what's to complain? Is Kopalski being squeezed out of the restaurant's ownership by his

*Ernst Lubitsch and Maurice Chevalier*     *Gloria Swanson and Billy Wilder (1950)*
*(1929) (Bison Archives)*             *(Alamy)*

neo-capitalist cohorts? Is it a cost-cutting measure to save on electricity? Or is Kopalski simply reveling in the individualism and free speech his escape from totalitarian tyranny have enabled?

A psychoanalytic reading might suggest that Kopalski, decidedly the shortest of the three unwise men, is indulging his Little Man complex, a theory supported by the less than imposing physical stature, not of co-writer Wilder—soon to become one of Hollywood's all-time greatest writer/directors *(Sunset Blvd., Some Like It Hot, The Apartment)*—but surely of the already legendary Ernst Lubitsch—noted for his risqué *(Trouble in Paradise)* and sometimes controversial (the anti-Nazi *To Be or Not to Be*) comic touch. [See Appendix A.]

More subversively, Kopalski's protest could be taken as a Marxist plea for the "little man" writ large—just the sort of leftist propaganda that Hollywood, in the McCarthy era, would be accused of having long slipped into its seemingly innocuous fare. As tantalizing as this second conflation of Freud and Marx might be, it collapses under the weight of the dream factory. For even if the seasoned Lubitsch and up-and-coming Wilder had let their leftist politics get the better of them, Louis B. Mayer or another MGM honcho would have nipped it in the bud. What *Ninotchka*'s counterintuitive conclusion ultimately leaves us with, then, is "narrative excess"—something in the story not fully explained or left dangling. Excess that circles back to actor/lothario Alexander Granach and the onlooker at the edge of the movie set whose coyness precipitated the scene within the scene—my mother, Eva Eger Bruch (later anglicized to Brook).

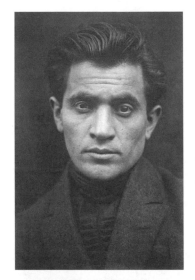

*Above left to right: 30-year-old Alexander Granach, and as Knock in the 1922 film* Nosferatu; *below left to right: Granach in the 1931 film* Kammeradschaft, *and as Mephisto in a stage production of* Faust. *(1, 3 and 4: Akademie der Künste, Granach-Archiv; 2: frame grab)*

CHAPTER 2

# "King of the Eastern Jews"

Not that Eva needed Granach's grandstanding to be impressed by the filming at legendary MGM studios. "*Und Lubitsch, mein Gott—und Garbo!*" she muttered to herself. "*Wenn meine Mutti mich jetzt bloß sehen könnte* (If only my momma could see me now)!" Nor did Granach really have anything to complain about. The illogic of the last scene notwithstanding, the actor got the last laugh. His face was the last one filmgoers would see, and his character's newly acquired underdog role even turned him, however incongruously, into *Ninotchka*'s unsung hero. So why all the *Sturm und Drang*?

Granach's loss of concentration in shooting the final scene may have been inadvertent, but there was method to the *meshugas* he made over it. The risk of being judged "difficult" and the cost over-run of an added take could easily be mitigated by a schnapps or two with fellow expatriates Lubitsch and Wilder. The tantrum even resonated with Granach's heyday as one of Berlin's leading actors in the 1920s, when, as director Berthold Viertel observed, "madness counted as nobler than common sense." Granach had starred in plays by Frank Wedekind, Ernst Toller, Georg Kaiser, Arnolt Bronnen, and Bertolt Brecht—prominent exponents of the Expressionst style that dominated theater and all the arts in Germany from the 1910s through the mid-1920s. And as a made-to-order Shylock—given his short, stocky frame and Hebe look—Granach, then in his early thirties, made his first splash in *The Merchant of Venice*, staged in 1921 by the celebrated Austrian-Jewish impresario Max Reinhardt. [See Appendix B.]

Granach's most famous film roles included Knock, the mad real estate agent (Renfield in the American vampire movies) in F. W.

*Max Reinhardt (1911) and Expressionist cinema* (The Cabinet of Dr. Caligari, *1920*)
*(1: George Grantham Bain Collection, Library of Congress; 2: Photofest)*

Murnau's inaugural Dracula feature *Nosferatu* (1922), and the miner Kasper in G. W. Pabst's antiwar drama *Kameradschaft* (*Comradeship*, 1931). But the stage was his forte, and where he became a *Liebling der Massen* (people's favorite) for his trademark "*Schrei*" (scream or shriek), which not only rose from the depths of his characters' souls but resonated with the rebellious zeitgeist and his own leftist politics. Perhaps the most potent aspect of Granach's appeal was the raw, ethnically inflected sexuality of his performances. As playwright Bronnen described, the "immense vitality of Eastern Judaism streamed out of him," inspiring his Weimar era nickname, *König der Ostjuden* (King of the Eastern Jews, "*juden*" pronounced "YOO-dn"). For while immigrant Ostjuden had long been denigrated in Germany, including by assimilated German Jews, as uncouth and backward (more about this internecine conflict to come), among sophisticates in the Weimar period, the Ostjude also came to be idealized as the "real" Jew, as opposed to the watered down, "denatured," German Jew. Among many Zionists and German-Jewish youth especially, the "cult of the Ostjuden," according to historian Steven Aschheim, became an "important expression" of their "rebellion against German-Jewish bourgeois life."

Nor was Granach's reputation lost on the host of Jewish émigrés among *Ninotchka*'s above-the-line personnel. Lubitsch and

Wilder, co-writer Walter Reisch, composer Werner Heymann, and Buljanov and Iranoff portrayers Felix Bressart and Sig Ruman were quite familiar with Granach's work. Indeed, having cut their teeth in Weimar-era Germany as well, they had experienced much of it first-hand. Greta Garbo herself, though neither German nor Jewish, might have rubbed shoulders with Granach during her pre-Hollywood stint at the UFA (Universum Film-AG) studio complex near Berlin, where he shot most of his films and she was starring in Pabst's *Die freudlose Gasse* (*Joyless Street*, 1925).

She would not, however, have been on hand for the filming of *Ninotchka*'s closing scene. This was a mere "pick-up," minus dialogue and shot MOS (an alleged acronym for "mitt-out sound," attributed to a German director's—possibly Lubitsch's—mangling of "without sound"). But Garbo's absence was no great loss to Granach. He had a pick-up of another sort in mind, and the Swedish coquette was its unlikely object. Her superstardom was no impediment, judging by his Weimar-era trysts with German leading ladies Helene Weigel (Brecht's wife) and the notorious Elisabeth Bergner (limned in the Prologue), among others. "The Berlin papers were filled with his

*Helene Weigel (1966) and Elisabeth Bergner (1935) (1: Photo: Hans Joachim Sprengberg/DLA-Marbach; 2: Public Domain) [See Appendix C.]*

escapades, scandals, and affairs," his son, Gad, recalled in his memoir *Heimat los!* (Homeless/Home lost, English title *Where Is Home?*)

Garbo's lesbian proclivities were another matter. But neither star power nor sexual orientation stood in the way with Eva Bruch. The closest she had come to stardom was the kneading of Hollywood celebrities' tired muscles, Granach's included. Their relationship most likely had begun on the portable massage table Eva carted to clients' homes for personal sessions, a table I remember fondly from the occasional massages she rewarded me with as a child. She'd landed the job thanks to a friend and fellow German-Jewish émigré, Gerda Weinman, a go-getter who had arrived in Los Angeles a few years before Eva. By catering to the growing colony of prominent escapees from Nazi Germany, for whom massage was second nature (sans sexual connotations) and the German language and cultural bond an added boon, Gerda had become a masseuse to the stars, non-German Charlie Chaplin among them. She later would marry a Dutch physician and acquire the name Goedhart, go recklessly sailing with him into the Pacific toward the end of World War II, be captured by the Japanese and imprisoned in the Philippines, become Bertolt Brecht's "court photographer" after the war, form a loving relationship with one of his ensemble actresses, Anna Blaman, and resettle with her in Vienna—but that's another story.

*A Dutch magazine featuring Gerda Weinman/Goedhart (De Parelduiker [The Pearl Diver], Issue 2010/3)*

In the late 1930s in Los Angeles, Gerda, given Eva's training in Germany as a physical therapist and her pleasing manner and appearance, asked her to join her thriving practice. Hollywood and California were magical names to Europeans in those days, and despite my mother's outwardly shy nature, her friend Gerda's offer sounded intriguing. By the time thirty-two-year-old Eva arrived in America on November 10, 1938, with her thirty-four-year-old husband, Rudy Bruch, it was an offer she couldn't refuse.

*A warning sign in 1933: "Germans! Beware! Don't buy from Jews!"—and a post-Kristallnacht synagogue (1: Bundesarchiv; 2: bpk/Abraham Pisarek)*

CHAPTER 3

# Kristallnacht

When my parents arrived at Ellis Island on November 10, 1938, Alexander Granach was a famous name from the Weimar period, but nothing more. Of far greater concern was the ghastly news that spread like a hissing snake along the lengthy line of immigrants waiting to be processed.

(Public Domain)

"*Hab ich's doch gesagt* (I told you so)!" Rudy exclaimed, visibly shaken as he handed a newspaper to Eva, who cupped a hand to her mouth as she read the shocking headline about a Nazi pogrom against Jews in Germany.

Holding back tears, she said almost in a whisper: "*Hoffentlich haben unsere Familien das alles überlebt* (Hopefully our families survived all this)!"

Rudy nodded with a sigh. "At least we got out in time. And maybe this will finally convince all German Jews, it's high time to leave as well!"

High time indeed. For November 10, 1938, wasn't just any date, especially for German Jewish émigrés. In fact, when my parents later told me and others about their arrival in America, I assumed they had fudged the date to make it sound more dramatic. But immigration records confirm their debarkation in New York City on the second of a two-day calamity since labeled *Kristallnacht* (literally "Crystal Night," aka "Night of the Broken Glass").

The name derived from the shattered glass of Jewish homes, businesses, synagogues, and schools sacked and burned to the ground in a Nazi-fomented, mob-driven rampage throughout Germany and recently annexed Austria. Besides the immense property damage—more than 250 synagogues and 7,000 businesses damaged or destroyed—Jewish cemeteries were desecrated and later filled with the scores of Jewish victims of the pogrom. Compounding the carnage and destruction and presaging the Holocaust, 30,000 Jewish men were rounded up and transported to prisons in Dachau, Buchenwald, and other concentration camps, where many perished.

Rudy's "I told you so" thus contained a maelstrom of mixed emotions, but it also spoke the truth. More politically astute than Eva, it was he who had convinced her of the urgent need to flee Germany even if it meant leaving loved ones behind and, as now seemed likely, in the lurch. He wasn't able to persuade her, however, to exchange a bourgeois life-style for his dream of joining a kibbutz in Palestine. So, after a stopover in Västraby, Sweden, where they both worked at a boarding school for refugee Jewish children until sponsorship could be secured and visas obtained, off to the New World they ventured—just in the nick of time.

Granach, meanwhile, who also arrived in New York in 1938, had an even closer call—and not only from the Nazis. Shut out of the film industry along with other Jews and leftists once Hitler came to power, his political activism placed him in an especially precarious position. Yet he "had the gall," his son, Gad, recalled in his memoir, to return to Berlin in 1933 to retrieve a year's back pay for his theater work. "With that he boarded the next plane to Switzerland. By midday the Gestapo had appeared at my mother's [Granach's divorced wife] apartment looking for him." In Switzerland he stayed for a while with his friend, Herman Hesse, the famed author and future Nobel Prize-winner in literature whose books *Siddhartha* and *Steppenwolf*

*Herman Hesse (1946) )*
*(Deutsche Fotothek)*

*Granach and Lotte Lieven (1925) (Akademie der*
*Künste, Granach-Archiv)*

would resonate strongly with the spiritual seekers of the 1960s. Perpetually drawn to the carnal as well as the spiritual, Granach also renewed relations with Lotte Lieven (more about her later), with whom he'd had an affair in Berlin and would form a lifelong (albeit long-distance) bond. But his Alpine stay was brief because, as history records, the 1981 West German film *Das Boot ist voll* (*The Boat Is Full*) reminded, and Gad dryly affirmed, "the Swiss response to exiles from Germany was hardly a model of compassion."

Next stop Poland, where, at least for a time, the Galician-born Granach was "something of a hero, as one of their own who had made it big in Germany." While in Warsaw, he started a Yiddish theater group and even gained some revenge on the Nazis with a successful production of Friederich Wolf's anti-anti-Semitic play *Die gelle Latte* (*The Yellow Patch*). Especially ironic, given his later role in *Ninotchka*, Granach, at the time a Communist and conversant in Russian, accepted an invitation in 1935 from the Kiev Yiddish Theater in Ukraine, then part of the USSR. There he met up with friends and fellow exiles from Berlin's theater and left-wing circles, among them Erwin Piscator and Bertolt Brecht, giants in the theater world for their writing and staging of plays and operas, and for their "epic theater" theoretical approach. [See Appendix D.]

*Erwin Piscator and Bertolt Brecht (1: Erwin-Piscator-Archiv; 2: Bundesarchiv)*

Besides his stage acting, Granach appeared in two Russian films, the anti-Nazi *Bortsy* (*The Fight*, 1936) and pro-Romani *Psoledniy tabor* (*Gypsies*, 1936). Then the other jackboot dropped. Caught up in the Great Purge of 1936–1938, Stalin's variation on the Nazi terror, Granach was branded "persona non grata" and jailed for "improper moral conduct"—where he languished until another noted German-Jewish refugee artist came to the rescue.

Novelist and playwright Lion Feuchtwanger, who had met Granach in Berlin, was then living in exile in France. Feuchtwanger had been labeled Public Enemy Number One by Hitler and would have his famous novel *Jud Süß* (*Süss the Jew*) turned into a virulently anti-Semitic film by the Nazis in 1940. But as an ardent leftist like Granach, he had ingratiated himself with Stalin during a celebrated visit to the Soviet Union in 1935. And the letter he now wrote Uncle Joe on the imprisoned Granach's behalf, together with a good word from Premier Vyacheslav Molotov's Jewish wife, Polina, secured Granach's eleventh-hour release and a safe exit from the country.

*Lion Feuchtwanger and the Molotovs (both 1930s) (1: USC Feuchtwanger Collection; 2: Fair Use)*

And thus it was that the famed, forty-eight-year-old actor made his still-treacherous way back through Switzerland (and Lotte Lieven) and on to the United States, arriving in spring 1938, a half-year before my parents. In New York he met up with his siblings and mother, all of whom, despite the country's restrictive immigration quotas, had managed to come to the United States already in the 1920s. He could rest somewhat easily about his son, Gad, as well, who had emigrated to Palestine in 1936, followed by his mother in 1937. But next to attractive women, acting was Granach's greatest passion, and not long after his arrival he was treading the boards again. The opportunity came thanks (and no thanks) to the Nazi-propelled exodus of European talent to America. The play, however, staged in New York in German by another noted Jewish exile, Leopold Jessner, failed at the box office. So, given his own émigré connections in Hollywood, trying his luck in the movie capital seemed the next logical step.

*Magdeburg on the Elbe (pre-World War II, exact date unknown)*

*The Allies' staged VE-Day handshake in Magdeburg, Western troops on the left, Soviets on the right (Alamy)*

## CHAPTER 4

# Writing on the Wall

Though Eva and Rudy sailed from Sweden together, they separated—and not for the first time—soon after landing in America. As I only learned much later as an adult, this and a similarly extended but temporary separation had preceded their departure from Sweden. Yet while a soothsayer might have predicted a tumultuous relationship by virtue of Rudy's surname Bruch (meaning "break" in German), my parents' "meet cute" in their pre-teens was worthy of a Hollywood romantic comedy.

They both grew up in Magdeburg, capital of the Prussian province of Saxony, roughly a hundred miles west of Berlin, where western and Soviet Allied troops momentously joined forces along the Elbe River in May 1945 to signal victory in Europe. The first of the world wars, ironically, had formed the backdrop for my parents' initial encounter in 1915. Both were then enrolled in the same Hebrew school class despite their age difference (he was eleven; she was nine), and as Rudy later recounted, "I fell immediately in love with a beautiful girl with long brown pigtails and blue eyes."

Problem was, how to get to the girl before Pincus—a rival for her affections, whom not only Rudy "but everyone in the class hated"—made a move. Problem solved, when Max, a precocious friend, gave Rudy, himself no shrinking violet, an idea.

"He suggested I should write on the blackboard: '*Eva ist süß, obwohl ich sie noch nicht gekostet habe*' (Eva is sweet, even though I haven't tasted her yet)."

Clearly not comprehending its off-color connotations, Eva was touched and amused, and proudly reported Rudy's bold stroke to

Rudy with his sister, Margot

Eva (in pigtails) with her sister, Ilse

her mother, Alma, who recorded her own reaction in her diary (here translated from the German):

"When I laughed and said, 'That certainly must be a very stupid boy!' Eva said, 'But why? He is very nice, and he is already eleven years old!' Next time, at *Sukkot* [the Jewish harvest festival in early autumn], she introduced him to me, and in front of the *sukkah* [the ritual holiday dwelling covered with foliage], he introduced himself in a very cute way. Indeed, an extremely charming and handsome young boy, Rudolf Bruch! He was very concerned that Eva get her piece of *challah* [a ritual bread served on the Jewish Sabbath and holidays] among the crowd, and he helped her taking off her hat, which bothered her. I enjoyed this all very much, because his attitude was quite childlike, yet gentlemanly. Since then, whenever she comes home from *shul* [the synagogue], she has to tell me something about Rudy. Yesterday, he even gave her a piece of challah to take home to Ilse [Eva's older sister]."

The writing, in other words, was on the wall, but it would take several years to materialize. Since Eva and Rudy lived in different parts of Magdeburg and went to different public schools, they saw each other only occasionally. Moreover, as Eva later explained in adulthood, though Rudy's solicitousness "was very important to my mother, it was not quite so important to me." Thus, while both she and Rudy joined the Jewish *Wanderbund* (hiking club) during their teenage years, their romantic roads, for the time being, diverged in a yellow wood.

The geographic distance, which along with the two-year age gap had hampered their relationship's more intimate turn as youngsters in Magdeburg, grew wider when Rudy left for Berlin to study law in the mid-1920s. This was the time of hyperinflation in postwar Germany, as illustrated in Rudy's later relating how his father, Oscar, a wholesale yardage salesman, had given his son what he thought was enough money to last him through the first semester in law school. But by the time he got to Berlin, the funds barely covered bus fare to the college dorm.

*A breadline in Germany in 1923 during the hyperinflation period (Bundesarchiv)*

Eva's tale of woe back in Magdeburg was one of hyper*de*flation, of an emotional rather than monetary kind. Personal tragedy had struck her and her family during World War I, not on the front but at home, when her mother, after a three-year bout with breast cancer, succumbed in 1918 when Eva was twelve. She recounted her mother's premature passing to me when I was a child, and it became a ritual of disclosure in her social encounters, like having to show your passport to get through customs. Later, in an autobiography workshop, she described in detail the tragic loss and its traumatic effects:

"When I was nine years old, the same year I met Rudy, and my sister Ilse was eleven, my mother Alma, who had just turned forty, had a mastectomy and one of her breasts was removed. Children in those days were kept in the dark about such things. So we had no idea of the seriousness of Mother's condition and its possible consequences. Besides which, she had always been rather frail and often fell ill, adding to our sense that the operation was nothing out of the ordinary.

"Ilse and I were very close to our mother. She spent more time with us than most mothers did with their children, and was very warm and compassionate. During World War I, she took us to military hospitals and brought sweets and cigarettes to the wounded soldiers. She was also quite artistic. She painted and decorated our rooms, designed and embroidered our dresses, told us stories she made up herself, and created plays for us to stage with our friends which the neighbors came to see. But the dresses stood out. I remember almost all *our* clothes, because Ilse and I were always dressed like twins.

"After her surgery, Mother received radiation treatment at a sanatorium in Braunlage, a resort town in the nearby Harz Mountains. But when the radiation gave her a rash, she was transferred to another sanatorium to treat the side effects, and when this still didn't help she was sent back to Sudenburger Krankenhaus, a local hospital in Magdeburg.

*Eva with her older sister, Ilse*

"Despite the physical and emotional strain, Mother kept up on all our activities and we sent letters and little poems back and forth. We also visited her often, but I didn't like to because of the depressing hospital atmosphere and the medicinal smells, which upset my stomach and prevented me from enjoying the 'special' food Mother had saved for us—omelets and pudding and other 'delicacies' that had become quite rare during the war. Another thing I hated about the hospital visits was seeing Mother with her hands bandaged, to keep her from scratching. But most disappointing of all was that after three months' treatment, her condition still hadn't improved.

"Finally some help came from Mother's brother, our Uncle Arthur Blumenthal, a physician in Berlin who arranged for treatment at the Ungersche Klinik in the city. This at least got rid of the rash, but the lengthy ordeal caused Mother to lose a lot of weight and undermined her overall health. So off she went to another sanatorium in Waltersdorfer Schleuse, a popular summer resort on the outskirts of Berlin. Ilse and I visited her there during *Pfingsten* (Whitsuntide, the holiday seven weeks after Easter celebrating the appearance of the

Holy Spirit to the apostles), and we were thrilled to hear she would be released in July, just in time for our summer vacation in Wieda, another nice resort in the Harz Mountains. I remember Mother

*Ilse, Eva, and their father, Hans, in happier times*

standing at the bus station at Waltersdorfer Schleuse smiling and waving good-bye. I didn't know this would be the last time we would see her.

"About a month later, in June 1918, Ilse and I came down with the Spanish flu, which, on top of the devastation of World War I, would turn into a worldwide epidemic and kill millions of people. One morning, while we were still in bed with a high fever, we heard Father come home early from work and start to pack his suitcase. A sudden shock ran through me, more powerful than any I'd had before or would ever experience again—'Mother is dead! This is the end!'—I realized. I prayed all night: 'Please God, don't let her die!' I promised to give up all my childish sins. But I knew it wouldn't help. She was gone. I would never see her again . . . except, maybe, in my dreams.

"Father only told us that he was going to Berlin, that Mother didn't feel well. 'I'll be back soon,' he said. Which he was, along with my mother's sister. But we knew already. A cousin of Mother's who lived in town had informed us. We cried bitterly, and Father tried to comfort us, but telling us he would care for us now, just the three of us, didn't help.

"That Ilse and I weren't able to attend the funeral because of our illness added to our sadness. As did the 'special' attention we received from the neighbors and teachers, as the two motherless little girls who had to tie black ribbons around our sleeves, a custom at the time for those in mourning. But worst of all was that all the pretty dresses Mother had made for us with such care, handstitched, with flowers and shiny ribbons, all these had to be dyed black as well. This practice made sense to me on a deeper level when I learned later that in English the words 'die' and 'dye' sound the same. At the time, it felt horrible for Ilse and me to have to wear our dear mother's blackened dresses. Not only because of the stain it put on her memory. It was like killing her all over again."

*Eva the artist: Self-portrait, 1924*

Deeply scarred by her dear mother's death, Eva dropped out of high school. She later enrolled in a *Frauenschule* (trade school for women), which she detested, but began to find her bearings in art school, where, like her mother, she demonstrated a gift for drawing. A career in art was a long shot, however, especially for women. So taking the advice, and financial support, from her father, Hans, who owned a small drugstore, Eva moved to Berlin to study gymnastics as a springboard to a possible teaching job.

*Eva the athlete, 1920s*

*Poster for* Berlin: Symphony of a Metropolis *(Photofest)*

Upon her arrival in the German capital in 1926, as underscored in Walter Ruttmann's popular documentary *Berlin: Die Sinfonie der Großstadt* (*Berlin: Symphony of a Metropolis*, released in 1927), the city was emerging from the economic and political turmoil of the early postwar period into the Weimar era's famed "golden age" of sensual thrills, sexual openness, and cultural stimulation. [See Appendix E.]

Despite all the distractions, after a two-year program at the Anna Herrmann Gymnastik Schule, Eva, then twenty-two, began teaching gymnastics and drawing at a local *Volkschule* (public primary school). Bolstered by the self-esteem her new job engendered, primed by the excitement of big-city life, and enabled by renewed proximity to Rudy, she began seeing her twenty-four-year-old former Hebrew school classmate again and, as she later wrote, "became closer."

## CHAPTER 5

# A Taste of Honey

"So *mein liebes Evchen* (So my dear Evie)," Rudy purred, as the reunited couple stood under a street lamp by the entrance gate to Eva's apartment house on a foggy Berlin night.

"*So mein lieber Rudolf,*" the normally shy Eva replied with surprising boldness, which he attributed to a combination of the bottle of wine they'd emptied at the local *Kneipe* (pub) and the film they'd gone to beforehand—*Pandora's Box*, G. W. Pabst's now classic 1929 adaptation of Frank Wedekind's pair of "Lulu" plays, *Erdgeist* (*Earth Spirit*, 1895) and *Die Büchse der Pandora* (*Pandora's Box*, 1904). Starring American actress Louise Brooks as the femme fatale par excellence, her seductive persona later moved French film historian

*Director G. W. Pabst (1949) (Alamy)*     *Louise Brooks as Lulu (Alamy)*

Henri Langlois to baldly declare, "There is no Garbo! There is no [Marlene] Dietrich! There is only Louise Brooks!" [See Appendix F.]

For Rudy, the emergence of Eva's Lulu side—wine-induced or not—emboldened him as well.

*Eva in her early twenties*

*Louise Brooks and Gustav Diessl in* Pandora's Box *(frame grab)*

"Can you believe it's been thirteen years since I wrote that silly thing on the blackboard?"

"Fourteen."

"I stand corrected."

"And it wasn't silly."

"It wasn't?" He drew closer and she waited until he was about to take her in his arms.

"It was *stupid*."

Taken aback—when she smiled he got the joke. "That's what your mother said, wasn't it? And you said, 'But Mommy, he's eleven years old!'"

They both chuckled.

"So who was right, me or my mother?"

"Who do you think?"

"I'm not sure. Maybe time will tell."

"I hope not another . . . fourteen years!"

"Absence makes the heart grow fonder."

"It has—at least for me."

She softened but remained tight-lipped.

"And I don't think I could go another fourteen years without"—inching closer—"finding out if Eva is as sweet as she seems."

"And how do you propose to do that?"

He gripped her waist and pulled her slowly towards him.

"By tasting her."

Their lips met, held a brief moment, politely parted—then merged more passionately.

"So?" she asked. "What's the verdict, counselor?"

He paused a moment, then recited, "How sweet are your lips to me! Sweeter than honey to my mouth!"

"A lawyer and a poet too."

"With a little help from King David."

"And a rabbi as well."

"No, but I think we might be needing one."

He leaned forward—but she pulled away.

"Not so fast, Rudolf Bruch!"

"I hope a little faster than fourteen years."

She smiled, opened the gate, shuffled to the apartment-house entrance, threw a Lulu-like glance back at Rudy, and disappeared.

"'Sweeter than honey to my mouth!'" he muttered to himself, recalling his ad-libbed paraphrase of Psalm 119. "Not bad for a 'stupid boy'!" he added with a Cheshire cat grin—then straightened up, clicked his heels, did a military left-face, and marched down the cobblestone street into the foggy night.

CHAPTER 6

# Pandora's Box

Pabst's *Pandora's Box* may have paved the way for Rudy and Eva's inaugural kiss, but for Germany and the rest of the world the film's early 1929 release was an eerie prelude to the evils unleashed later that same year by the Wall Street Crash on October 29. Flashforward two years to my parents' Jewish wedding on October 24, 1931, in Magdeburg—where outside the festooned *chuppah* (marriage canopy)

Weimar's golden age had already devolved into the Depression-era chaos that would propel the Nazis to power. Indeed, had Pabst, after directing Granach in 1931's *Kameradschaft*, filmed the Bruchs' wedding ("Bruch," remember, meaning "break"), a ceremony-ending close-up of the ritual glass-breaking (sym-bolizing the destruction of the

*"If I should forget thee, O Jerusalem, let my arm forget its cunning..." (Photo: Jacob Engelhart)*

Temple in Jerusalem, which Jews are bidden to recall even in their happiest moments) would have literally foreshadowed Kristallnacht and its prelude to the Holocaust.

Such a foreboding image could have served as a metaphor, as well, for the strains on a young German-Jewish couple in the years leading up to the Night of Broken Glass. Partly from a hope-ful, "this too shall pass" attitude shared by many anti-Nazis (until Kristallnacht), and having no credentials to build on in a foreign land as did Granach and other noted artists and intellectuals, Rudy

*A hotel in modern-day Norderney (2018, above) and (left) President and former General Paul von Hindenburg appointing Hitler Chancellor on January 30, 1933 (1: Dietmar Rabich/Wikimedia Commons/"Norderney, Weststrand, Hotel—2018—1050"/CC BY-SA 4.0; 2: Alamy)*

and Eva joined the legions of "stay behinds" through Hitler's ascension. Despite the dire conditions, in little over a year between their marriage and the Nazis' power grab, the newlyweds (then twenty-six and twenty-eight) managed to weather the larger financial crisis, even with Rudy still in law school. Thanks to Eva's success as a teacher and promotion from a part-time to a permanent member of the faculty at a progressive school on the nearby Frisian island of Norderney, she later wrote, "*von meiner Einkommen könnten wir gut leben* (from my income we were able to live well)."

"*Dann kam Hitler* (then came Hitler)," she added, and all bets were off.

Even before President von Hindenburg's death in August 1934, after which parliament was dissolved and Hitler appointed *Führer und Reichskanzler* (Leader and Chancellor), the Nazis not only set out to get the trains running on time and the economy back on its feet. They also immediately began implementing the 25-point platform devised in 1920 by the party's forerunner, the NSDAP (*Nazional Sozialistische Arbeiter Partei*, or National Socialist Workers' Party), whose overarching goal was to segregate Germany's Jews, deny their civil rights, and exclude them from public life. The most draconian of the NSDAP's measures were inscribed in the Nuremberg Laws of 1935, which revoked Jews' German citizenship, nullified their right to vote or hold public office, and prohibited intermarriage or sexual relations with non-Jews. Already in 1933, however, besides their banishment from the film and media industries, Jews had been expelled from the civil service, and their participation in the medical and legal fields was sharply reduced. In major cities, including Berlin, Jewish legal services were eliminated entirely, which meant that Rudy, once he finally finished his studies and passed the *Assessor* (Bar) exam, was unable to practice law.

Eva fared somewhat better. Though education hadn't been spared in the Nazis' anti-Semitic decrees, which imposed strict quotas on Jewish enrollment in public schools and universities, the pioneering founder of Eva's school in Norderney, Gertrud Feiertag, turned an obstacle into an opportunity. She had relocated the school in 1931 to a converted villa in Caputh (pronounced Kah-POOT), a charming village outside Potsdam near Berlin where Albert Einstein had spent summers with his wife, Elsa, from 1929 to 1932. After the Nazi takeover in 1933, Einstein, who was then in the United States and would never return to Germany, arranged for the rental of his summer house to Feiertag, who converted it into the dormitory where Tom Tugend resided during the student days he describes in the Foreword. The dormitory was confiscated by the Nazis in 1935, but fortunately not the school. Instead, Feiertag's *Jüdische Kinder und Landschulheim* (Jewish children's boarding school) remained a

*Gertrud Feiertag and her Jewish school in Caputh (Ingeborg Papenfuss)*

refuge for less fortunate Jews and children of leftist political parents (often one and the same), who along with Romanis, homosexuals, and the disabled had also become targets of Nazi persecution.

Rudy wasn't left completely in the cold. Always dreaming of becoming an opera singer, he joined a short-lived singing troupe, *"Die Zwanzige Jüdische Sänger"* (the Twenty Jewish Singers), a touring company of professionals likewise forced out of their chosen fields by the Nazis. Unable to make the cut as one of the tenors, Rudy became the troupe's booking agent, and after its dissolution parlayed his administrative experience, a winning personality, and his marriage to Eva into a part-time clerical job at Feiertag's Jewish boarding school.

For a nature lover like my father, the school's idyllic location alone was a boon. Tucked in the the dense woods of Potsdamer Forest beside the sparkling waters of Caputher Lake, the school's comparative isolation and distance from the big city made it an oasis in more ways than one—buffering it from the hubbub of the German capital and, as one of the Nazis' *"vergessene"* (forgotten) schools, shielding it (for a time) from undue government scrutiny. His additional salary also allowed the Bruchs to squirrel away some savings.

Affiliation with a progressive, Zionist-sponsored institution also meshed with Rudy's political ideals. And most of all, the comparatively undemanding office job allowed him to do some work on the side with *Hechalutz* (the Pioneer), the leading Zionist organization, headquartered in Berlin and charged with promoting emigration to Palestine.

Hechalutz lived up to its "pioneer" name both as the first major organization of the early Zionist movement and in its training of Jewish youth to break ground (literally, through agricultural work) on what they hoped would become a new Jewish homeland in Palestine. An offshoot of Hechalutz, called *Hachsharah* (Preparation), would enable Granach's son, Gad, to emigrate to Palestine. After the First Zionist Congress (held in Basel, Switzerland, in 1897) made the Theodor Herzl-inspired movement official, Hechalutz, founded in the greater New York City area in 1905, gave it practical footing. Zionist impetus increased exponentially

*Modest Stein, photographer, 1930*

with the Balfour Declaration of 1917, named for British Foreign Secretary Lord Arthur Balfour, which proclaimed British support for "a national home for the Jewish people." Hechalutz subsequently opened branches throughout the United States, Canada, Europe, and Russia, and at its peak in the 1930s had expanded to South America, North Africa, and the Middle East. At the onset of World War II, the group totaled 100,000 members worldwide, with some 60,000 having already moved to Palestine. Shortly after Israel's founding in 1948, Hechalutz was absorbed into the more militant *Hashomer Hatzair* (the Young Guard).

*A demonstration by the ultra-Orthodox sect Neturei Karta, in New York City in 2010 (Alamy)*

## CHAPTER 7

# Bruch's List, Part 1

**W**hile Granach was hailed as a hero in Poland and continued to perform on stage and screen there and later in the Soviet Union, Rudy, in the mid-1930s, as he recounted in a taped conversation with me in 1983, "became a high-ranking member of Hechalutz, and my task was to propose candidates for receiving visas to Palestine. The British, who controlled Palestine at that time, granted admission only to very few single applicants, but many more to couples. So to save as many as possible, I arranged for thousands of marriages. I had whole lists of people and tried to match them as best I could, age-wise, background-wise, and so on. One case was particularly bizarre. I got a letter from Yugoslavia saying they had twenty young girls for the program. Now you can imagine their names—Anrolova, Pipapova, and the like—and I had to change all these names to match the German names of the men they were to be coupled with. Which I managed to do and they all left and made it to Palestine.

"One exception I made was with *Agudat Yisrael* (Union of Israel), whose members I was in a position to pass over and I did. This wasn't easy, because most Agudat Yisraelis were from Hessen, the agricultural heart of Germany, and so they qualified as agricultural workers and were therefore entitled, but I turned them down. This may sound harsh, but I felt strongly, and still feel, that my actions were justified.

"Agudat Yisrael was an ultra-Orthodox party founded in direct and vehement opposition to the Zionist movement, because they believed the formation of a Jewish state should occur only after the arrival of the Messiah. Fundamentalist Christians, of course, believe just the opposite—that the founding of Israel heralds the Second Coming. But besides Agudat Yisrael's theological opposition, they sent people to Palestine with the express intent of preventing the establishment of a Jewish state by any means necessary. As much or more than the Arabs, in other words, Agudat Yisrael was Zionism's mortal enemy. Now I myself have since [by the early 1980s] become quite critical of Israeli policies, but I stop short of anti-Zionism, which *Neturei Karta* (Guardians of the City)—an offshoot of Agudat Yisrael formed in 1938 and with members living in Israel today— still holds to. Other, though by no means all, ultra-Orthodox, on the other hand—ironically and I would say hypocritically—have become among the staunchest of Israel's rightwing supporters!

"Then I was arrested." Rudy paused here for dramatic effect, before resuming his oral history.

"The circumstances were the following. In one weak, over-worked moment, I dictated a letter to my secretary, which dealt with the application of a Jew living in Palestine who had tuberculosis. The question was whether the German government would allow him to come to Germany for a cure, and would guarantee his return to Palestine. I had written one letter already and gotten no answer. Finally, from exhaustion and frustration, I dictated another letter threatening to seek assistance at a higher government level if no answer was forthcoming. I got my answer. They wrote back that I was '*unverschämt*'—impertinent—and called me at 9:30 that same morning and told me to be prepared to go straight to the police station and to prison!

"Now it so happened that this very day I had in my possession a large sum of money (the equivalent of about $60,000 today), which I was supposed to deliver that same evening to a man from *Haganah* (the Defense) at a certain *Konditerei* (bakery). Haganah was the main Jewish paramilitary organization in Palestine, which I was also involved with at the time. After the establishment of Israel in the late 1940s, Haganah became part of the Israeli Defense Forces. But back in the 1930s when I held my bag of money intended for

*Haganah fighters (Palmach Archive) [See Appendix G.]*

Haganah, had the German police who came to the house to arrest me found any of it, I wouldn't be sitting here today. Fortunately, their forewarning gave me the chance to call somebody else from Hechalutz to deliver the money for me. But I still had to pay for my impertinence.

"So I was taken into *Schutzhaft* (protective custody), and in a way I wouldn't have missed it. It was a great experience. I was put into a large cell along with twenty-four others at its peak. It wasn't always that full, but over the weekend we got all the drunks, the Seventh Day Adventists, the socialists, the homosexuals—it was just a frantic scene. There was one guy, a thief, and the Seventh Day Adventists argued with him, saying he wouldn't go to Heaven. And he shot back, 'I'll go to Heaven, all right. *Wo ick die zehn tausend Paar Bemberg seidene Strümpfe gestolen habe, müssen sie auch gewesen sind.*' In Berlin dialect that translates roughly as: 'If I stole ten thousand pair of fancy silk stockings, you can bet they were there to begin with'— meaning that he only stole from the rich.

*A detail photo from a 2018 revival of the play* Bent *(Martin Sherman, 1979), about the persecution of gays in Nazi Germany, who were made to wear pink triangles in the concentration camps, similar to the yellow stars of David that Jews were forced to wear. (Photo: Alisabeth Von Presley/Theatre Cedar Rapids, 2018)*

"There was one homosexual, the son of a wealthy Rhinish industrialist, very good-looking, and I'll never forget his tie. It was most unusual for the time—bright, riotously colorful, with broad stripes. And every afternoon they let him out on entrapment patrol, to act as bait. He would stand at a certain known pick-up spot and whoever made advances got nabbed. Then we had a transvestite, also dressed colorfully and with black silk panties. He made us laugh and was very popular. But if anyone asked him to take off his breasts, he got huffy and said that was going too far. Of course he had other reasons to be upset. The Nazis treated gays almost as badly as the Jews, and they also died in great numbers in the Holocaust." [See Appendix H.]

Rudy paused here again, as if out of respect for the gays he had known in Germany and the likely tragedies that befell them. "As I look back on my own thankfully brief prison experience," he continued, "the whole thing was a circus—though not always enjoyably. For one thing, none of us knew if we'd ever get out. And I as a Jew was particularly anxious, as was Eva. Given the precariousness of the situation, we developed a code system in which, in our correspondence, Eva referred to me by another name. And one day she received a letter from the authorities saying that the person with my code name would soon be seeing her again. And sure enough, a few days later I was released."

*Haavara Agreement transfers (Palmach Archive)*

# Bruch's List, Part 2

The most bizarre aspect of Rudy's prison stay, at least in retrospect, wasn't the carnival atmosphere or the comical way he describes it. Most absurd, and bitterly ironic, is that except for acting as a go-between for Haganah, his other activities with Hechalutz hadn't been illegal. All his marriage arranging with Hechalutz, which, according to Rudy, like Oskar Schindler's efforts, saved thousands of Jewish lives, was done with the full knowledge and approval of the Nazis.

Prior to settling on the Final Solution at the Wannsee Conference in 1942, Hitler had toyed with various less lethal means of solving the so-called "Jewish question," including expulsion and voluntary migration. The most notorious scheme was the Madagascar Plan, first floated by Poland in 1937 and by Germany in 1940, which proposed relocating the remaining Jewish populations in Nazi-occupied territory to the African island of Madagascar, a French colony ceded to the Germans after the fall of France. Already in 1933, however, the Nazi regime had entered into the so-called *Haavara* (transfer) Agreement with the Zionist Federation of Germany and the Anglo-Palestine Bank, which sanctioned German-Jewish migration to Palestine. It was under Haavara's guidelines that Rudy's marriage lists were compiled and overall, circa 60,000 Jews, between 1933 and 1939, were granted visas to Palestine.

Far from a humanitarian concession by the Nazis, Haavara served their *"Judenrein"* (Jewish purging, or ethnic cleansing) policy while also boosting the country's GDP via the stipulation that all emigrant assets be used to purchase goods manufactured in Germany for export to Palestine. The Zionists, meanwhile, gained more than just a compassionate pat on the back. The *Yishuv* (Jewish community in Palestine) reaped multiple economic benefits through the influx of immigrant labor and essential goods the agreement enabled. Though they may have been pawns in a geopolitical game at the time, the greatest beneficiaries in the long run were the Jewish immigrants themselves, whose timely move to Palestine likely averted their later transport to the death camps. Not all the Haavara-spared Jews, however, including those resulting from Rudy's arranged marriages, avoided hardship upon resettlement in the Promised Land, as he himself observed first-hand in the late 1930s and also related to me in our taped conversation.

"The tragic thing about some of my efforts I saw myself when I went to Palestine with a group of *Halutzim* (Zionist pioneers) as a transport leader, and I met many of the couples I had matched up. For in those days getting divorced there was no easy matter, and maybe even impossible (because under strict Jewish law, a husband could reject his wife's divorce request). So, naturally, some of the couples were happy together, in some cases one of them was happy, and in others neither of them was happy. But they were stuck. It was very tragic!"

"Now wait a minute, Dad!" I felt like interjecting. "The exchange of a torturous death for a bad marriage—very tragic?!" This notion struck me as quite strange at the time, but I kept the puzzlement to myself. Only after his death, not long after our conversation in 1983, did I learn of a possible explanation—namely, that Rudy's own marriage had seen better days by the mid-1930s. The hardships and anxiety of the Nazi period surely contributed to the conjugal conflict. And for those inclined toward name symbolism, the Bruch moniker once again didn't help. No matter—or worse yet—that it was likely a Germanization of the Hebrew "*Baruch*," meaning "blessed." But deeper fissures in my parents' relationship also began to surface, and would reemerge later in America.

Historical, linguistic, and relational factors aside, in the Nazi period the sticking point, as with Rudy's mismatched marriages, was Palestine—given his passionate desire to settle there, and Eva's equally staunch opposition to the prospect. And so, as the situation for Jews in Germany became increasingly dire, and the need to make evacuation plans increasingly urgent, the Bruchs' unresolved conflict over "making *Aliyah*" (immigrating to the Land of Israel) precipitated their first major separation as a married couple.

In 1937, when Rudy left for Västraby, Sweden, the stopover point for his and Eva's eventual emigration to America, he went alone, and not with the New World in mind but the Promised Land. Västraby was a logical first step, partly because, through Hechalutz, temporary employment awaited him at Kristinehov Internat, the Jewish boarding school where Eva also would later be employed. The primary enticement, however, were the adult horticulture classes the Zionist-oriented school offered, along with other preparation for immigration to Palestine.

Eva initially remained in Germany—not only for lack of Zionist fervor and aversion to the hardscrabble life it held in store. She also was loathe to leave her father, Hans, and sister, Ilse, now with a Christian husband, Karl Meyer, and their young child, Peter. Not that Rudy's parting from his own mother and sister, Elise and Margot, and ailing father, Oscar (who would die of natural causes in early 1938), was a guiltless decision. But his finer-tuned political antenna, and his recent brush with Nazi authorities, reinforced a now-or-never sense of the need to leave Deutschland.

*Eva's father, Hans Eger*

Three factors led Eva to finally come around, not to Rudy's kibbutznik dream, but to the plausibility and exigency of emigration. The job Gerda Weinman had dangled in California made America a solid alternative to Palestine as a safe haven. Ilse's having a Christian husband increased the odds of their

*Eva's sister, Ilse, and her husband, Karl Meyer*

*Ilse and her newborn son, Peter*

*Rudy with his sister, Margot*

*Rudy's mother, Elise Bruch*

family's surviving the Nazi terror (which they miraculously man-aged to do). And events at Gertrud Feiertag's school in Caputh were turning warnings of that terror's full-blown eruption from alarmist speculation to increasing certainty.

CHAPTER 9

# *Alles Geht Caputh*
# (Everything Goes "Kaput")

The 2002 documentary *Prisoner of Paradise* tells the tragic tale of Granach's fellow actor during the Weimar era, Kurt Gerron, who went from co-starring with Marlene Dietrich and Emil Jannings in *The Blue Angel* (1931) to being sent to the Theresienstadt (Terezín, in Czech) concentration camp and from there to Auschwitz in 1944, where he and his wife were gassed. Compounding the tragedy is Gerron's having abetted—with the promise that he'd be saved—the Nazis' promotion of Theresienstadt as a "model" camp where Jews were allegedly well treated and content. His part in the devilish ruse consisted of writing and directing (together with Czech film-maker Karel Pečený under Nazi supervision) a short documentary titled *Der Führer schenkt den Juden eine Stadt* (*The Führer Gives a City to the Jews*). The film presented the prison much like a summer camp or resort and "featured," among other diabolical performances, a children's opera, *Brundibar*, and jazz-band leader Martin Roman and his Ghetto Swingers. Roman survived the Kafkaesque

*Kurt Gerron and Theresienstadt camp (frame grabs)*

## THE AFRO AMERICAN
### NATIONAL
45th Year, No. 45.    BALTIMORE, MD., AUGUST 8, 1936    Price: 10 Cents

# "ADOLF" SNUBS U.S. LADS

*Clockwise from left: Jesse Owens, an African American newspaper's slap at Hitler, and Helene Mayer saluting the Führer (1 and 3: Public Domain; 2: The Afro-American)*

grotesquerie, but the children and most of the musicians suffered the same fate as the Gerrons.

The Jüdische Kinder and Landschulheim Caputh was subjected to a similar, if less lethal, ignominy. During the 1936 Olympics in Berlin, Nazi racial theory, though dealt a blow in African American Jesse Owens' and other black athletes' record-breaking performances, prevailed in Hitler's snubbing of Owens and allowing only one German athlete, whose father was Jewish, to compete—fencer Helene Mayer, who went on to win a silver medal and dutifully gave the Sieg Heil. Elsewhere, a carefully stage-managed, Potemkin Village impression of interracial harmony reigned, and the Jewish school in Caputh served as a poster child for the subterfuge.

Guided by Nazi-trained personnel, foreign delegations received a less flagrantly fabricated tour of the Jewish school in 1936 than International Red Cross observers were given of the Theresienstadt camp in 1944. In the latter case, well-clothed and seemingly healthy incarcerated adults, and children smiling from a one-off ice-cream treat and other goodies, were showcased (and filmed by Gerron), before being shunted back to their tattered clothes, cattle-like stalls, and starvation diets.

The children in Caputh actually enjoyed, for a few years and except for obligatory schoolwork and light chores, an almost fairy-tale existence, as Tom Tugend recalled in the Foreword. What was wrong with the picture, during the early Hitler period, lay mainly beyond the frame and behind the scenes. The Nazis for years had been harassing the school administration, limiting and sometimes rejecting group activities, and draining its resources through higher taxes than were imposed on non-Jewish schools. Then, starting in 1935, no doubt spurred by the draconian Nuremberg Laws, things turned ugly. Einstein's summer house, which had become one of the school's dormitories, was confiscated. Hostile encounters with Hitler Youth, such as Tom Tugend experienced, occurred in broad daylight. And at night, unidentified belligerents began sporadically hurling stones that shattered the school's windows—terrifying and flagrantly criminal acts that Feiertag reported to the police, to no avail.

*Dann kam Kristallnacht.*

Rudy and Eva, by a stroke of fortune and my father's good sense, managed to avoid this catastrophe. But not the news, communicated

*Jewish children given rare treats in Gerron's film about life in Theresienstadt (frame grabs)*

*Rendering by a Theresienstadt inmate, Leo Haas, titled "Children on the Way to Auschwitz," as depicted in* Prisoner of Paradise *(frame grab; Ben Uri Gallery and Museum)*

later by friends and relatives, that the Landschulheim was among the Jewish properties decimated during Kristallnacht. Especially harrowing, and galling, was the fact that teachers and students from Caputh's non-Jewish schools, along with other "upstanding" members of the community (no doubt including the aforementioned Hitler Youth and stone-throwers), avidly lent a hand to this Gestapo-led foreshadowing of the Holocaust.

News of the Kristallnacht calamity at the Jewish school in Caputh, which reached my parents soon after their arrival in the New World, only compounded their concern for their close relatives left behind in the Old. Just before embarking for America, Rudy and Eva had met Ilse, Karl, and young Peter in Lund, Sweden, a site chosen to allow for a final farewell between them. Peter, in a memoir written as an adult decades later, explained another motivation:

"My father's being Christian was the only reason we managed to survive at all in Nazi Germany during the war—then only barely, and always underground. Already before the war he had tried to have me baptized as a precaution, but the priest in Magdeburg refused to perform the ceremony because of my Jewish mother. So when I was two-and-half years old, we all went to Sweden, where my mother's sister, Eva, and her husband, Rudy, were staying on their way to America. They acted as my godparents when I was baptized in the historic Lund Cathedral (featured twenty years later in Ingmar Bergman's *Wild Strawberries*).

"Eva and Rudy pleaded with my parents to come with them to America. But my mother couldn't bear leaving behind her and Eva's aging father, Hans Eger. In the end, neither my mother nor anyone else could save him. On November 18, 1942, he was sent by transport number XX/1-18 to the 'model' concentration camp in Theresienstadt, where he died on January 20, 1943. In a final bitter irony, his cremated remains were strewn into the nearby River Eger that bears his name. By no means done out of respect, the Nazis had begun disposing the ashes of the deceased in this manner late in the war to cover up their misdeeds.

"I knew nothing of my beloved grandfather's perishing in the Holocaust, or that he, like my mother, was Jewish, until after the war. This information was kept secret from me and my two younger brothers for obvious reasons. Instead my parents pretended—through all the hardships they were forced to endure—that our family had nothing out of the ordinary to fear."

*The Eger River (Ohře, in Czech), and Peter Meyer with Grandpa Hans Eger (1: CC BY-SA 3.0, Orange man)*

Peter eventually immigrated to America in 1951 when he was sixteen, together with his eleven-year-old brother, Michael. Peter lived for a time with our family in the San Fernando Valley and Michael stayed with our neighbors, the Odenheimers, a fellow

German-Jewish refugee family whose mother, Dorothea (called "Doro"), had taught with Eva in Caputh and whose father, Fred, would work briefly as a gardener's helper with Rudy. Peter and Michael's arrival was the hoped-for first stage of a transfer to America of the entire Meyer family, my only close living relatives, which by then also included Peter and Michael's younger brothers, eight-year-old Christian and five-year-old Tommi. Unfortunately, because the Soviets had appointed my Uncle Karl, a pre-Nazi era Social Democrat, mayor of the Soviet

*Left to right: Christian, Tommi, Peter, and Michael Meyer, shortly before Peter and Michael immigrated to America (courtesy Miriam Meyer)*

sector city of Domersleben for a short time after the war, he was denied entry to the United States during the McCarthy era, and thus he and the rest of the family remained in West Germany. Karl and Ilse eventually visited America, but never became permanent residents. Tommi and Christian did, however, and all four boys went on to earn PhDs, raise families, and have successful careers.

The youngest son, Tommi, recalls only beginning to grasp what it meant to be part Jewish when he was eight years old. His father prompted this greater understanding when he arranged a string-quartet version of a Hanukkah song, which Tommi (second violin), Christian (cello), Michael (first violin), and Karl (viola) played in a rabbi's home in Bonn—Beethoven's birthplace and the West

German capital (until reunification), where the Meyers then lived. Despite this new awareness, and though no one in the family was a churchgoer, Tommi and Christian chose to be baptized when Tommi was eleven and Christian was fourteen. The ritual's main allure, at least for Tommi—as the bar and bat mitzvah have become for many Jewish young-sters—was the prospect of gifts and money on the other end. Michael was never baptized, and married a Jewish woman,

*Peter celebrating Christmas*

Miriam Herschorn (more about her family in Chapter 11). Peter later acknowledged, with considerable regret, that it wasn't until in the early 2000s, after visiting Theresienstadt where his grandfather had died, that he finally fully identified with his Jewishness.

*Eva in happier, and more troubled times (dates unknown)*

## CHAPTER 10

# Baggage Claim

"**W**hy *that* far away? Why not go to Holland?" Eva's doctor advised her in early 1938, upon hearing of her planned move to America. And, at the time, his counsel wasn't altogether unsound. For though "the need for survival and my youth" prodded Eva into taking this quantum leap, the thought of an ocean-bound journey to a far-off land with a foreign tongue (most of the Dutch also spoke German) was understandably terrifying for a thirty-two-year-old woman whose reunion with Rudy in nearby Sweden would already prove a daunting adventure. "Before I left my homeland I had nightmares," she later wrote. "I saw strange and scary objects flying high up in the sky to an unknown, mysterious place, and I was puzzled and terribly frightened."

One can only imagine the nightmares that followed news of the Final Solution that began filtering through to the Allied countries from 1942 on, and the excruciating anxiety caused by the near impossibility of learning the fate of loved ones in Germany until after the war. Eva's sister, Ilse, had been informed during the war, through a letter to their father, Hans, of Rudy's mother's and sister's deportation to a transit camp in Izbica, Poland, in March 1942, and apparent death from starvation soon thereafter. She amazingly also had learned, through a letter tossed by a fellow inmate over the Theresienstadt camp walls and put in a mailbox by a passerby, of Hans's death there in January 1943. Immediately conveying this tragic news to my parents, however, was another matter. Thus, the final blow for them, with survivor guilt heaped onto bottomless grief, most likely was delayed until after VE-Day. Nor would this have

*Feiertag's former school, now the Jugendhilfezentrum (youth services center) Gertrud Feiertag (Axel Hindemith, Creative Commons CC-by-sa-3.0 de)*

been the end of the postwar, Holocaust-related death notices, which among their close friends included that of Gertrud Feiertag. Soon after Kristallnacht she had moved to Berlin and helped out with the *Kindertransport* of Jewish children from Germany, even accompanying one group to England, where she could have remained. Instead, fatefully, she returned to Berlin to continue her humanitarian efforts. These lasted well into the wartime period and ended, along with her life, after her transport by the Nazis to Auschwitz in 1942. Her gassing there in 1943 snuffed out the founder, but not the heroic legacy, of her Kinder und Landschulheim Caputh, which has since been renovated, commemorated, and is once again in operation.

Well before my parents' wartime and postwar psychological pummeling, ample grounds for apprehension already existed. This included post-Kristallnacht concern for those left behind and, first and foremost, their own material means of survival as strangers in a strange land. Whether the situation was as dire as Eva's cliché-sounding claim, "*Wir kamen hier mit nur zehn Dollar an* (We arrived here with only ten dollars)," finding regular employment was surely a top priority. Eva, of course, had a job as a masseuse ready and waiting in Los Angeles, with train fare west supplied as an advance by Gerda Weinman. Rudy, however, would remain in New York—not because he lacked a job or transportation expenses, which he did. But because he and Eva, shortly after their arrival in the U.S., separated for the second time in little over a year.

Eva later told me, after Rudy's death in 1983, that Separation #2 was mainly her doing. She didn't specify why, but I assumed it was because Rudy's compromising on the migration to Palestine hadn't resolved their underlying relational issues, and the move to America hadn't made them magically disappear. As I'm partial proof, they eventually would subside. In the meantime, as crestfallen as he must have been at the Bruch moniker once again living up to its name (and another reason to change it to Brook!), a movie-industry connection, as it did for Eva, at least helped put a roof overhead and bread on the table.

German-Jewish and American stage and screen actress Lotte Palfi Andor (née Mosbacher) had emigrated to the United States in 1934 with her first husband, actor (and later film editor) Victor Palfi, with whom my parents (and I as well) would later become good friends in Los Angeles. Upon her divorce from Victor, and with little luck finding film work, Lotte turned to the stage in New

Lotte Andor in Casablanca (*frame grab*) and in Marathon Man (*frame grab*)

York, where she resided upon Rudy and Eva's Kristallnacht arrival. Eventually she would gain some revenge on the Nazis in a series of films: *Confessions of a Nazi Spy* (1939), the first openly anti-Nazi film by a major Hollywood studio; *Casablanca* (1943), the most famous of all anti-Nazi films; and *Marathon Man* (1976), in which she had a feature role as the elderly Jewish Holocaust survivor who spots Lawrence Olivier's Mengele-like doctor and screams epithets at him as she chases him through the streets of modern-day Manhattan. [See Appendix I.]

*Rudy the gung-ho gardener*

Through Lotte, with whom Rudy had become acquainted via his Zionist work in Berlin, he managed to obtain room and board in New York, with payment derived from the typical fresh-off-the-boat jobs of dishwasher and the like. Most important for his future return to middle-class status, he also took horticulture classes and found occasional gardening work. The instruction and hands-on experience built on the horticulture classes he'd taken in Sweden, directed toward his hoped-for move to Palestine. The increased expertise and self-confidence he gained in New York, with an additional boost from Hollywood yet to come, would eventually spur his upward mobility in America.

## CHAPTER 11

# The Medium is the Massage

Granach was still in New York when the Bruchs arrived on Kristallnacht, and his stay would overlap with the first few months of Rudy's early gardening days there. In March 1939, however, still struggling to make his mark on stage, he learned of the planned MGM production of *Ninotchka*, starring Greta Garbo. He knew of Garbo's relationship with Salka Viertel, an actress friend from his Berlin days and a fellow Galician Jew, who had become a screen-writer on several of Garbo's films, her trusted confidant, and, rumor had it, also her lover. So he wrote Salka in Hollywood and asked, ever so humbly, whether there might be a part in *Ninotchka* for someone who "could firstly (what could I not?), play any role!" and "secondly, could provide you with a bag full of experiences." Next thing you know, the King of the Eastern Jews, following his life's topsy-turvy pattern, was on his way to Los Angeles, landing a plum supporting role in *Ninotchka*, and, coincidentally—a cushy spot on Eva Bruch's massage table.

Eva's friend, Gerda Weinman, hadn't located her clinic in Hollywood by chance. The site's appeal stemmed not only from the deep pockets of the movie people who lived and worked in the area, but also from the large number of recently arrived Jewish émigrés among them. This "second wave" of Hollywood Jewish exiles from Nazi Germany, moreover, was culturally inclined to view massage quite differently from the "first wave" that had fled persecution in Eastern Europe at the turn of the nineteenth century and helped establish the movie industry, as well as from most Americans at that time. Rather than a rare luxury or an activity reserved primarily to

*Three faces of Eva*

treat bodily pain or injury, massage was taken more for granted, much as yoga is by many today, as part of a routine physical fitness regimen.

Besides Swedish massage, Gerda's practice offered pregnancy and nerve-point techniques, all of which Eva needed some additional training to perform. Canny entrepreneur that she was, Gerda had taken this delay into account, trusting that the gymnastics exercises Eva was well-equipped to supervise, both before and after a brief training period, would actually add to the clinic's overall appeal. And indeed, it was on the exercise floor, not the massage table, that Eva Bruch and Alexander Granach first made their acquaintance.

The stretching movements she demonstrated in a flimsy blouse and shorts to a small group of mainly middle-aged men and women showcased her well-toned, somewhat boyish figure. The "Vun-too-sree, vun-too-sree!" she barked with Prussian authority (and accent) in their calisthenics routine revealed less a drill sergeant than a sheep in wolf's clothing. She still possessed the striking combination of brown hair and blue eyes that had entranced eleven-year-old Rudy, and her appearance was updated through the morphing of her pigtails into a close-cropped cut similar to, and possibly inspired by, the China-doll style of *Pandora's Box* star Louise Brooks. Eva's comely physique, pixyish good looks, and quasi-innocence would have proven irresistible in any case for a consummate Casanova like Granach. When combined with the isolation, intimacy, and innuendo of the massage table, to which she quickly graduated, their affair was all but foreordained.

As has long been recognized and exploited, the erotic potential of massage is inherent to a form of physical therapy based on full-body contact. Less frequently acknowledged is the *psycho*-sexual dimension—the release of tension and anxiety facilitated by a reclining position analogous to and likely partial inspiration for the psychoanalyst's couch. A crucial difference between the two therapies is that the masseuse, unlike the analyst, is free to engage in casual conversation whose loosening of the tongue enhances catharsis for the client, first and foremost, but can prove infectious for the masseuse as well. And for the Don Juan, the uninhibited verbal exchange only added to his arsenal of aphrodisiacs, allowing him to turn the tables on both Freud and the masseuse by not only wondering but helping determine "what the woman wants."

*Alexander Granach (Becker & Maass, Berlin)*

A built-in ice-breaker for the thirty-three-year-old Eva and for-ty-nine-year-old Granach was their shared German-speaking/Jewish background and émigré status. The commonality served his seduction strategy further by allowing him to play up his celebrity as a famous Weimar-era actor soon to appear in *Ninotchka* without making him seem too out of reach. But the trump card was his "powerful personality," and sexuality, whose Eastern Jewish eroticism had endeared him to Berlin audiences and helped inspire the "cult of the Ostjude." As Miriam Rochlin, who came to know my family in Los

Angeles and had known Granach well in Berlin, described him in an interview: "He was terrific!"

Eva had sensed Granach's animal magnetism on the exercise floor, but his attraction broadened during their massage sessions, when he turned on his legendary charm and directed their increasingly intimate conversation toward her feminine instincts.

"The earth in East Galicia where I was born is prodigal and rich," he began his life story with all the theatricality he could muster, cribbing the words from an autobiography he had been drafting and that would be published some years later. "It spouts forth black oil, and bears golden tobacco, and grain as heavy as lead, and old dreamy woods, and rivers, and lakes, and above all, handsome healthy men. Men admittedly somewhat slow but good-natured, a little lazy, but fruitful like their mother earth."

The segue from self-deprecation to virility and, most importantly, the poetic language, besides showcasing Granach's sensitivity and charisma, were also calculated to overcome, or at least to mitigate, the persistent divide he sensed between the "cultured" *Westjude* (Western European Jew, pronounced "VEST-yooduh") and "primitive" Ostjude with the peasant face and "crooked baker's legs" (since straightened in an operation). The Weimar-era idealization of the Ostjude, spearheaded by Zionists and German-Jewish youth, had always been compromised by the failure of German Jews to acknowledge the basic humanity of the idolized "other." In any case, the adulation had already worn thin during the Nazi period and was an even poorer fit in 1930s Los Angeles. By then the overall relationship between Ost and Westjuden had reverted to one of "brothers and strangers," as Steven Aschheim aptly described it—even among fellow émigrés who were now essentially in the same boat. That this schizoid dynamic lasted well beyond World War II, I sadly witnessed with my own Zionist father. An otherwise open-minded, unbigoted man, when it came to Ostjuden—such as my cousin-in-law Miriam Meyer's parents—while he acted politely toward them in person, behind their backs his attitude reverted to one of haughty disdain.

*Stereotypical Ostjuden (Alamy) and a definitive Westjude, Lion Feuchtwanger (USC Feuchtwanger Collection)*

Eva, similarly, though she was not about to display anti-Ostjuden animus in her working relationships, couldn't help but share its historical roots. The longstanding gulf between the Ashkenazi (European Jewish) cousins, based in large part on the economic and cultural disparity of their respective regions, was widened by the emancipation decrees of the late eighteenth and early nineteenth centuries. Inspired by the French Revolution and initiated first in France and soon thereafter in other Western European countries, the new laws granted previously ghettoized Westjuden entry into mainstream German society while leaving their Ostjuden co-religionists stranded in Polish shtetls and the Russian Pale of Settlement. The massive migration in the late 1800s and early 1900s of Ostjuden to Western Europe, and eventually the United States, by thrusting the two groups together and highlighting their differences, exacerbated the rift between them. In Germany, the "backwardness," traditional Orthodoxy, and general poverty of the Ostjuden immigrants not only threatened to undermine the Westjuden's hard-won, if still only partial, upward mobility. It was also a painful reminder of their own ghetto roots.

Thus Granach had to tread carefully through this mine-laden terrain, relying on his celebrity, sexuality, and the occasional Jewish joke—related in German and with Hollywood as its butt—to both

*Adolph Zukor (1914) [See Appendix J.]*

defuse, and use to his advantage, the intra-ethnic tension.

"Just look at MGM, and all the major studios. All run by Hungarian Jews, Polish Jews, Russian Jews, just like me. Now back in Vienna and Berlin, the creative people, the movie-makers, like Lubitsch and Billy Wilder, they all looked down on these filthy peasants and shop-keepers from Eastern Europe. But when they got to Hollywood, what happened? The shoe was on the other foot! They got a taste of their own medicine! ... Or as Billy put it, 'We went from Adolf Hitler to Adolph Zukor!'"

"Who is Adolph Zukor?" Eva asked.

"The filthy shopkeeper who heads Paramount Pictures."

## CHAPTER 12

# One-downsmanship

It didn't take long for Eva to relate to Granach the tragic story of her mother's death, which, as mentioned earlier, was a calling-card compulsion of hers. Yet for the purpose of his massage-table courting, her painful disclosure was an added perk: allowing him to display genuine sympathy with her plight and to segue seamlessly to his own childhood tale of woe. Not to minimize Eva's suffering, but his own youth, given an upbringing mired in poverty and unmarked by class privilege, arguably had been even more agonizing than hers. Granach could even point to a mother who almost died *before* he was born, as his parents had come close to divorcing just prior to his conception. Materially, the tribulations began in infancy, as

Granach visiting his mother on the Eastern Front in 1914 (Akademie der Künste, Granach-Archiv)

part of a family of nine children raised on a meagre farm in abject squalor, all sleeping together in two small rooms (when not in the barn during summer), and with one "chief worry: not enough to eat."

Testing the Yiddish motto "*Meschane mokim, meschane mazl*" (Change your place and you change your luck), the family moved when Alexander was five from their village of Werbiwci to the town

*Galician Jews, 1886 [See Appendix K.]*

*Galicia during the Austrian Empire period (1804–1867)*

of Skolje. Both were part of Galicia, then (in the 1890s) an Austro-Hungarian province populated mainly by Poles and Ukrainians but with a sizeable Jewish minority. And while the Skolje match factory provided work for Granach's father and all the children over eight, and helped put food on the table, before long even this comparative good fortune turned into a curse.

After only a few days, from the chemicals used to make the matches, "everything in the house ... our food, our bread, our clothes, our wash ... stank of sulphur and phosphorous." Most of the family "began to look pale and to have pains in the joints," with two of the children "becoming knock-kneed."

Then anti-Semitism came knocking.

The Polish patriarch of a neighboring family welcomed the Granachs with a drunken ditty: "The Jew, the Jew, the mangy Jew! I found his hat—and what did I do? I shit in it—and so would you. Now he'll have to buy a new!" After another swig or two, the lyrics turned lethal: "When I drink schnapps, I have a Jew for a *zakuska* [to eat after it]." The neighbor's older sons added injury to insult by knocking the younger Granach children off their sleds, beating them up, and running away laughing.

Alexander's father—a pious man "who knew the Talmud and could quote the whole Bible from memory"—defied both the timid

Jewish stereotype and Jesus's "other cheek" dictum by giving the bigoted neighbor a thrashing of his own. But when the Granachs tried to leave town, they were stopped by police and ordered to return. Papa Granach had the final word, though, telling the mayor, "You can't do anything to a man who merely objects to seeing his children become cripples," but this victory proved pyrrhic.

Upon the family's next move to the district seat of Horodenka, signs on house after house greeted them "with a black stripe drawn in coal which meant—TYPHUS!" Soon there was one on the Granachs' lintel "and the entire household lay ill with fever and chills."

The wild hallucinations Alexander suffered—of armies of giant, green-bellied lice crawling across his naked body while he lay

*A Dutch poster for the Nazi propaganda film* Der Ewige Jude (The Eternal Jew, *1940) (frame grab) and a cartoon from an August 27, 1939, edition of the prewar, anti-Semitic Polish newspaper* Samoobrona Narodu (Self Defense of the Nation). *The visual metaphor clearly draws on the* Dolchstoss *(German for "stab-in-the-back") accusation made against Jews in Germany during and after World War I, a canard that built on longstanding European questioning of Jewish patriotism and contributed greatly to the Nazis' rise.*

paralyzed and unable to move a muscle or cry out for help—were anything but. When he finally woke from the real-life nightmare, the fever had broken but not the hunger that accompanied it. Both he and his brother, famished beyond constraint, began stealing loaves of bread and, pangs of guilt notwithstanding—"We stole and ate and ate and stole and thus secretly fed ourselves back to health."

Once out of the musty room and able to take in his new surroundings, the precocious Alexander gained insights that would mold his later worldview. Horodenka—a town as different from the village of Werbiwci as the town itself was from any European capital—had introduced the young boy not only to a terrifying disease of the physical body but also to an equally perilous and more widespread sickness of the body politic.

There had been poor and rich in Werbiwci, "and hail and drought and pestilence," he recalled. "But such things were everyone's concern, and people were close to one another and helped one another." Horodenka was built on and riven by class division. The town's outer circle was most like Werbiwci, semi-rural and impoverished. In the center, home to the middle and upper classes, one "began to see villa-like houses." And in between, "hedged in by these two circles, lived the Jews." Defying the ghetto stereotype and mirroring the town at large, the Jewish quarter was divided in two as well. One section was comparatively well-off, housing the wealthier merchants, agents, and financiers. The other was dirty and stank, "and when no rain or frost came to wash away the filth and clean the air, people were simply suffocated." You can guess where the Granachs lived, but still managed to survive.

## CHAPTER 13

# Riffkele

Survival of the fittest was Horodenka's Social Darwinist motto, at which six-year-old Alexander proved himself remarkably adept. Unlike Schabse, his seven-year-old brother and partner in crime during the typhus outbreak, whose inability to master the "evil traits of city people," the "rivalry and greed," caused him to sink deeper into insecurity, Alexander's self-confidence soared. His quick study of the town's dog-eat-dog philosophy also set Alexander apart from his parents, whose foray into the bakery business, from "no steady clientele... did not prosper." Alexander, meanwhile, amassed a windfall on the side hawking *kvass* (apple cider sweetened according to a local peddler's secret formula). Drawing attention to himself by singing loud curses at the peddler, who gouged them, he managed to outsell his meek older brother by two-thirds and won his father's praise for chutzpah—a quality he likewise displayed in *cheder* (Hebrew school).

At least that's how Rabbi Schimshale cannily interpreted his young charge's brashness. A weary, bearded old man, whom Alexander and the other boys had initially taunted, Schimshale eventually won more than their trust. "We loved our haggard and wonderful rabbi-teacher. He was sacred to us as the Torah itself, someone for whom you would do absolutely anything." So when the rabbi told Alexander, who continued to be a terror outside class, "You are braver and smarter than the others—and just for that reason, you should protect them and not frighten them," he succeeded in tempering Alexander's baser instincts, at least as a one-off favor to his beloved mentor.

Public school was another story. Here the harsh discipline—"the teachers treated us like little animals and beat us"—provoked rather than tamed Alexander's delinquency. His classmates also reveled in committing pranks on the teachers and outside school formed a gang engaged in petty thievery, with Alexander in the lead. A part closer to those he would later perform on stage and screen was inspired by a travelling circus troupe, whose main attraction was the tightrope act of a young boy. Having marveled at the cheering crowd and the boy's bravado, Alexander, back home in the bakery, engaged in perhaps his first acting role. Teetering on a mockup of a highwire, he aped the boy's cry—"Father, the wind!"—before a packed house of admiring neighbors and other townsfolk.

By the time Alexander turned ten, five of his older brothers had already left home, through marriage or to seek other opportunities. "So the family became smaller and smaller, but our poverty grew greater." Yet when the bakery finally went under, the bankruptcy actually benefited Alexander, whose new job at a rival bakery further boosted his independent streak, and his interest in the opposite sex as well.

A slender fourteen-year-old, "poor and simple" with "firm, round curves, snow-white skin, silky brown hair, large dark burning eyes, and two dimples in her firm little face," Riffkele was Alexander's first love. He met her delivering bread to her family one early morning in Zaleszczyki, a small town along the Dniester River, and was so struck by her that he got a baker's job in the town to be near her.

Alexander, however, was not yet thirteen—a "fifty-center," as Riffkele's nineteen-year-old boyfriend, "Curl," mockingly called him. Eventually, the rival swains came to blows, which ended in a toss-up and "made them square." To no avail, as Riffkele ultimately moved to another village and spurned Curl as well. But the whole experience—of being on his own, of earning his keep, and suffering his first major heartbreak—taught Alexander more than a doctoral degree might have, an older Russian friend, Czerniakoff, told him. "Because life is hard and merciless, it teaches and forms and kneads, just as you knead your dough."

## CHAPTER 14

# From Malka to Lemberg

"Just as you're kneading me now," Granach murmured, as Eva ran her supple fingers down his spine.

"Well, I wouldn't go that far, Herr Granach," Eva replied. "I like you, but *need* you?"

Granach glanced back to see if Eva was being facetious, and when she smiled coyly, he let out a hearty laugh.

"So what happened next, Herr Granach?"

"*Alexander*, please!"

She smiled broadly and began stroking his shoulders.

Things were progressing nicely, he thought. Revealing one's inner life creates a special bond. Of course his story wasn't free of embellishments, and omissions. He wisely passed over his relationship with a prostitute in Stanislau, the city he'd moved to shortly after the misadventure with Riffkele, where his brother Leibzi lived and another bakery job was available. Instead he emphasized his religious piety at the time, of having dutifully performed, in the early morning after a long night's work, the Jewish ritual of putting on *teffilin* (phylacteries)—two small black leather boxes containing verses from the Torah.

*A Jewish youth performing the teffilin ritual, derived from Deuteronomy 6:8: "And these words which I command you today shall be in your heart. And you shall bind them as a sign upon your hand, and they shall be a reminder between your eyes." (Alamy)*

As shown in the photo, these are bound to the forehead and to an upper arm, and the verses are recited during weekday morning prayer services.

The bakery provided a less reverential reminder of his Jewishness, considering the pejorative name given to the low-rung job he started out with: *"jidl"* (little Jew). But it was Malka he had on his mind when Eva began digging into the ridges of his shoulder blades. He'd met Malka after losing his baker's job, and apartment, during a strike in the dead of winter. His bar mitzvah in political activism bolstered his manhood in other ways when he found shelter at Herr Bretzele's brothel. After a few days of cringing in a corner, one of the girls, "a full-bosomed, wide-hipped woman with a three-story red hairdo," took pity on the penniless teenager and let him bed down in her room across the street.

Besides his gratitude and physical attraction to Malka, Alexander couldn't help but feel sympathy for her as well. A Romanian Jew, she had been disowned by her parents for having a child by a *goy* (Yiddish and Hebrew for gentile). Then the goy deserted her and the child, and Malka, to spare her daughter a childhood in a brothel, left her with another family but continued to support her. Over time Alexander became a fixture at Herr Bretzele's, doing odd jobs and even serving as a bouncer. The trust he earned with Malka was rewarded one night when she undressed and jumped into bed with him, after which, he recalled in his autobiography, "Now I was a man—her man! And she was my first wife."

The honeymoon didn't last long. When Alexander struck up a friendship with a younger prostitute, their purely platonic relationship didn't placate Malka, whose intense jealousy finally drove him away. Along with his brother Leibzi, who bought him a train ticket to the truly big city of Lemberg (today part of Ukraine and called Lviv), the capital of Galicia with an even larger percentage and wealthier class of Jews—which is where he picked up his life story with Eva.

He was now once again together with two older brothers, Leibzi and Abraham, and spent alternate months staying at each of their homes. They taught him how to dress and coif more suitably for a big city, and advised him to abandon the "swinging gait" modeled on Herr Bretzele's (clearing his throat) "men about town." Altogether, he became "a new man, in new surroundings, and began a new life." Yet while the appearance and surroundings may have been novel, Alexander's baker's job had become a deadening routine. And even Lemberg, with all its tumult and size a hundred times bigger than Horodenka, had "nothing that surprised me, nothing to make me wonder. But one evening..."

Eva flinched and pulled her hands away as Granach's neck muscles suddenly tightened. "One evening we went to the theater! And there I found something different...another world, an unknown, a new world...a hundred times more exciting than the most exciting dream!" Beyond the thrilling spectacle of it all, the reverence the theatergoers displayed toward the actors reminded Alexander of the adulation of the ultra-Orthodox in Horodenka for the wonder rabbis. The whole experience was revelatory, and Alexander's curiosity, the master trait that had propelled all his actions, "began to itch in the region of my heart." This was the world where he belonged, the road he was destined to travel, and "within me there was now a silent, iron resolve to walk that road! To force my way into that world...and no power on earth could keep me back or block the road into that world for me!"

*Pacific Palisades section of the New Weimar (Photo: Michael Locke)*

## CHAPTER 15

# The New Weimar

**G**ranach now had Eva in the palm of his hand. But she was a delicate flower, and some tending of the bloom was required before tasting its sweet nectar. And he had just the right tool: the European-style salon, one of which Granach himself had hosted during the Weimar period. "There was always something exciting going on at his place," his son, Gad, reported. "The apartment would be full of people: writers, philosophers, actors"—among the writers, Bertolt Brecht, Herman Hesse, and Thomas Mann's novelist brother, Heinrich Mann; among the actors, Heinrich George and past, present, or future paramours, Helene Weigel and Elisabeth Bergner.

Transported to their alien refuge in Los Angeles, these *kaffee-klatsch* cum cultural gatherings served two additional functions—as support group and occupational network. As the salons had in Europe, the Southern California variant existed on both the lofty artistic and more mundane planes. Among the latter type was a get-together of former lawyers, doctors, other professionals, and their spouses, formed in the early 1940s and called *die Gruppe* (the group). Rudy and Eva eventually became regular Gruppe members and Granach attended as a guest of honor.

At the high-end salons Granach took Eva to in 1939 while Rudy was still in New York, the famous actor was just one of the crowd. Hosted mainly by the wives of prominent artists and intellectuals in their often opulent homes, with guest lists featuring the cream of the European cultural elite, these assemblies of primarily German and Austrian Jews eventually lent sobriquets such as Ghetto under Pacific Palms, Weimar by the Sea, and New Weimar to the affluent

Westside section of Los Angeles along the Southern California coast where the bulk of the celebrity salons were held.

Émigré notables besides Granach one might find schmoozing or performing on a weekend at any of a half-dozen New Weimar salons included the aforementioned writers Brecht, the Mann brothers, and Lion Feuchtwanger; composers Igor Stravinsky and Arnold Schoenberg; philosophers Theodor Adorno and Max Horkheimer; architects Rudolph Schindler and Richard Neutra; impresario Max Reinhardt and his screenwriter/producer son Gottfried; film stars Greta Garbo, Marlene Dietrich, and Peter Lorre; and filmmakers Ernst Lubitsch, Billy Wilder, and Fritz Lang. Non-Continental European luminaries enjoying the *Sachertorte*, *Apfelstrudel*, and stimulating conversation included Charlie Chaplin, Frida Kahlo, Diego Rivera, Frank Lloyd Wright, Edward Weston, and John Cage, among many others.

Though an eclectic mix dropped in on the refugee salons, their more regular frequenters tended to reflect the particular *salonnière*'s, or her husband's, specific cultural orientation. Thus the most popular of the gatherings, hosted by Granach's old friend and his entrée to Hollywood, Salka Viertel, wife of director Berthold Viertel, tilted toward movie people. Those of Marta Feuchtwanger and Nelly Mann, Heinrich's wife, leaned toward writers. Painter/art patron Galka Scheyer's favored fine artists, photographers, and architects. And artist muse Alma Mahler Gropius Werfel attracted a mix of composers, architects, and novelists like those she had married—Gustav Mahler, Walter Gropius, and Franz Werfel. A prize catch, indeed, which Tom Lehrer satirized in the 1960s with his now classic lyric: "Alma, tell us—all modern women are jealous. Which of your magical wands, got you Gustav and Walter and Franz?"

Granach gravitated toward the Salka Viertel salon, partly for professional purposes. He also, of course, owed Salka enormous gratitude for helping him get the part in *Ninotchka*. But he introduced Eva to some of the other salons as well, and after the Feuchtwangers' arrival in the early 1940s, made a pilgrimage to their sumptuous

*Marta Feuchtwanger (1920s) (USC Feuchtwanger Collection)*

*Salka Viertel (date unknown) (DLA-Marbach)*

*Galka Scheyer (1930s) (Norton Simon Museum)*

*Alma Mahler (1909/10) (Alamy)*

Pacific Palisades home (named Villa Aurora), from even greater gratitude. Upon first sight of the famed novelist, wife Marta recalled, Granach "fell on his knees before him" and said to her—recalling Lion's letter to Stalin on his behalf—"This is the man who saved my life." Besides his own last-minute reprieve, Granach was well aware of the Feuchtwangers equally perilous escape from the Nazis.

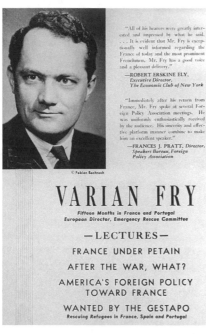

"All of his hearers were greatly interested and impressed by what he said. . . . It is evident that Mr. Fry is exceptionally well informed regarding the France of today and the most prominent Frenchmen. Mr. Fry has a good voice and a pleasant delivery."
—ROBERT ERSKINE ELY,
*Executive Director,*
*The Economic Club of New York*

"Immediately after his return from France, Mr. Fry spoke at several Foreign Policy Association meetings. He was uniformly enthusiastically received by the audience. His sincerity and effective platform manner combine to make him an excellent speaker."
—FRANCES J. PRATT, *Director,*
*Speakers Bureau, Foreign*
*Policy Association*

© Fabian Bachrach

## VARIAN FRY

Fifteen Months in France and Portugal
European Director, Emergency Rescue Committee

—LECTURES—

FRANCE UNDER PETAIN

AFTER THE WAR, WHAT?

AMERICA'S FOREIGN POLICY
TOWARD FRANCE

WANTED BY THE GESTAPO
*Rescuing Refugees in France, Spain and Portugal*

*(U.S. Holocaust Memorial Museum)*

A thorn in Hitler's side well before the Führer's coming to power, and having his German citizenship revoked already in 1933, Lion and Marta had fled first to France. When this haven proved short-lived, Lion's intervention with Stalin initially forestalled his own entry to the then more anti-Communist than anti-Nazi United States. Finally, via American journalist Varian Fry's famed wartime refugee network (which ultimately saved thousands, including Heinrich and Nelly Mann, and Franz and Alma Werfel, the couple made their way in 1941 across the Pyrenees, then through Spain and Portugal and on to the United States, eventually settling in tony Pacific Palisades. [See Appendix L.]

An upscale coastal community carved into the Santa Monica Mountains, Pacific Palisades, prior to the influx of European émigrés, had been home to a wide range of settlers once the native Gabrieleño Indians (so named for the Mission San Gabriel they were consigned to) had been dispossessed and displaced. In the 1910s, pioneer movie producer Thomas Ince built Inceville, one of the first major West Coast studios, a stone's throw from the ocean and just below the Feuchtwangers' eventual hilltop home. In the

1920s, a planned Methodist commune put down stakes in the area. And in the 1930s, a wave of émigrés made the beachside communities the New Weimar hub. Little did they know that their idyllic

*The Feuchtwangers, and their Villa Aurora (USC Feuchtwanger Collection)*

sanctuary from the German Jew-haters now lay cheek by jowl with Murphy Ranch, an underground American Nazi base tucked away in the same coastal foothills.

Started by the Silver Legion and manned by so-called Silver Shirts, this and other domestic fascist groups, with the movie capital as their main focus, were dedicated to facilitating—by any means necessary—Hitler's hoped-for world conquest. Their terrorist plots, chillingly detailed in Steven Ross's book *Hitler in Los Angeles*, included infiltrating the film and defense industries (the former successfully, the latter

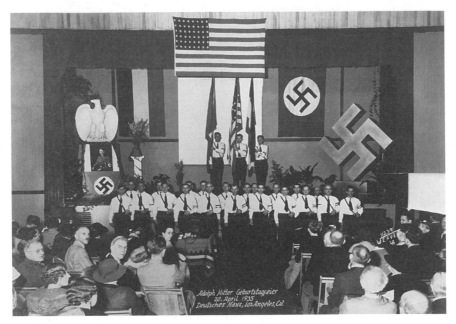

*Celebrating Hitler's birthday in Los Angeles, 1935 (Fair Use)*

*Murphy Ranch ruins, 2006 (CC 2.0 Generic, Arthur Robinson) [See Appendix I.]*

less so), bombing military installations, and assassinating Jews (both thankfully thwarted).

Granach's designs on Eva, of course, were more modest and humane. But by hook or by crook, the Old and New Weimar lothario was determined to make the Magdeburg masseuse his own.

## CHAPTER 16

# Trouble in Paradise

When Granach led Eva across the threshold of Salka Viertel's salon at 165 North Mabery Road in Santa Monica, she couldn't in her wildest dreams have imagined that someday she, too, would live in an elegant Westside abode—and, of all places, situated just above the Feuchtwangers' Villa Aurora. On that autumn evening in 1939, however, she couldn't fully enjoy the fairytale surroundings or Salka Viertel's prestigious company.

A creative spirit but no intellectual, Eva felt out of place at the high-end salons Granach introduced her to. She shared a German-Jewish émigré background with many of the cultured guests, but little else. And while she ran into another massage client here and there, as if to compensate for the intimacy they shared in the therapeutic environment, their exchanges in this social setting reverted to bromides and pleasantries.

Salka Viertel's former house, in 2019 (Photo: Michael Locke)

The guest Eva felt most comfortable with, surprisingly, was the notoriously haughty and morose film director Fritz Lang, a monocled fixture at Salka Viertel's salons. [See Appendix M.] When accompanied by his vivacious wife, Lilly Latté, Lang more easily

*Fritz Lang (1960s)*
*(Alamy)*

blended in. Otherwise, as Salka Viertel's son, novelist and screenwriter Peter Viertel, recalled, "He seemed remote, unapproachable, sitting off by himself and nursing his martini. Distinctly uncomfortable in the group setting, he always behaved with meticulous formality." Around Eva, however, his Germanic gruffness softened and they shared some light banter, until Granach, no doubt intuiting in Lang some of his own womanizing proclivity, would whisk her off.

"He's a Nazi at heart, you know," Granach muttered.

"I thought he was a Jew," Eva demurred.

"Lilly is. And Lang's mother was. But she converted to Catholicism."

"That doesn't make him a Nazi."

"Goebbels asked him to head the film industry!"

"But he refused."

"Only for Lilly's sake."

Eva still liked Lang. And she was flattered by Granach's jealousy. What weighed on her at the moment, more than her social discomfort, was her balance sheet. Her massage work, while an obvious hit with Granach, had fared less well with her other clients, as she herself sensed and Gerda Weinman, however tactfully, conceded. Also, though she appreciated the slice of paradise Granach had granted her access to, and enjoyed the attention he lavished on her (by then extending to the bedroom), she was worldly enough to surmise that their relationship was destined to be short term. Once his Hollywood career took off, which it was primed to do after *Ninotchka*, some starlet was sure to take her place. Nor would having a child, which was increasingly on Eva's mind (and her biological clock was ticking), likely have much appeal for Granach, whose only offspring, Gad, he'd sired over twenty years earlier with his then-wife, Martha Guttmann.

*Granach with son Gad in 1920s Berlin (Akademie der Künste, Granach-Archiv)*

*Getting it both ways?*

Thus Eva's thoughts began to wander eastward. She knew from their correspondence that Rudy, her legal husband, was still in love with her and also just getting by. But asking him to rejoin her in Los Angeles was only part of her plan. For behind her shy exterior, as Rudy noted (but didn't fully grasp) on the night of their post-*Pandora's Box* kiss in Berlin, lurked a Lulu. And so along with a rapprochement with Rudy, Eva also, as long as her Hollywood lover would have her, didn't want to let the charming (and virile) Granach go.

Balancing the affair with a return to married life would of course require some fancy footwork. Not so much with the bohemian Granach, whose manner suggested and salon gossip affirmed he was neither the marrying type nor averse to an affair with a married woman. The challenge was keeping the more monogamously minded Rudy in the dark. Getting him to cross the continent wasn't a problem. Besides the torch he still held for her and the preternatural allure of sunny California, the offer to "taste her again" came sweetened with the prospect of lucrative gardening work. This possibility Eva had gleaned from salon mate Fritz Lang, who happened to be in the market for a new gardener, a field then dominated in Los Angeles (until FDR's wartime internment order) by the Japanese.

*Japanese versus Mediterranean style landscaping (Photos: Michael Locke)*

"Now I have nothing against the Japanese," Lang protested a bit too much, but he did have a point. "They're reliable and conscientious, but they're not really gardeners, just maintenance men. A mower, a rake, and a hose, *c'est tout*. And if they do know something about landscaping, it tends toward the more formal and austere Japanese style, not the Mediterranean style that lends itself to this region and which I prefer."

Rudy, on the other hand, having honed his horticultural skills for the past year in New York, and with his German background to boot, was made to order for Lang. And with Lang's hoped-for recommendations, plus Eva's massage clients and their connections, who knows how far Rudy's gardening business might go in La La Land?

## CHAPTER 17

# Auld Lang Syne

"Fritz Lang drove me crazy," Rudy later recalled in our taped conversation. "He was known as a sadist. There's a story about how he forced Peter Lorre, whom he made famous in the role of the child murderer in *M*, to fall down a staircase seven times—not to get the scene right but out of pure sadism.

"He could also be very charming, but finally I couldn't stand him. He was very demanding, had his own ideas. I did learn from him to love the oleander, that colorful shrub that lines many of the Southern California highways, and which is also quite poisonous. It was his favorite plant, from his early days in Italy. And through him I got a lot of my first gardening jobs. At one time or other I had just about the whole German colony of refugee artists and intellectuals as my customers, many involved in the movies. Besides Lang and

*Peter Lorre in* M *(1931) (Photofest)*

later Peter Lorre himself, a few of the others were director Douglas Sirk, who became very popular in the 1950s with social melodramas, actress Elisabeth Bergner, a big star in the Weimar era, and actress and singer Hildegard Knef, who starred on Broadway in *Silk Stockings*, the Cole Porter musical based on *Ninotchka*. One of my favorites was ... "

"Now wait a minute, Dad! Is that all you have to say about Bergner and *Ninotchka*?!"—at least this again is how I might have interrupted our conversation, had I known in 1983 of Granach's affair with Bergner, which I only learned about during my research for this memoir. But what I really wish I had broached, for which the Bergner affair provided the perfect opening and which I *was* aware of at the time, was Granach's affair with Eva. Trudy Dresdner, a close friend of the family's, had told me about it just a few years before. She had divulged it to me in confidence, and thus I hadn't brought up the matter with either of my parents then, and I didn't do so in my conversation with Rudy. Today, with the wisdom of hindsight, I wish that I had, along with mentioning Granach's romance with Bergner, who had been— Eva, Lotte Lieven, and all the actor's other paramours notwithstanding—"the great love of his life." This bit of gossip, again, comes from Granach's son, Gad, who added, "My father never really got over her. He had many women in his life, but she would remain a taboo subject not to be mentioned." I wonder how Rudy might have reacted to this new information, and whether it might have altered—for good or ill—his feelings toward the man who, as we'll see, would play such a disruptive role in my parents' marriage and our family's life.

But in 1983 I bit my tongue and Rudy simply continued listing his impressive clientele. "One of my favorites was novelist and screenwriter Vicki Baum (wife of conductor Richard Lehrt), who wrote the bestseller that became the Oscar-winning *Grand Hotel* (1932), starring Greta Garbo. Vicki had a great feeling for plants and sent me a long letter describing how she wanted her garden landscaped.

"Not all my clients were émigrés. And some I got through the Jewish Employment Service. In fact, since Lang had to give his old

*Douglas Sirk (1978), Hildegard Knef (1969), Vicki Baum (1960) (1: Alamy; 2: Nationaal Archief: Erich Koch/Anefo; 3: Nationaal Archief: Anefo)*

gardener notice before hiring me, my first job was through the Jewish Service, as a helper on a big estate in Beverly Hills, bordering the Harold Lloyd estate. It consisted of about seven acres of hillside lawn, and I didn't yet have a power mower, much less a truck and tools. And every morning I had to get there by bus and mow a part of the lawn and put the cuttings along the fence bordering Harold Lloyd's place.

*Harold Lloyd (1924) and his timeless image from* Safety Last! *(1927) (Public Domain)*

"One nice thing was that when I got to the fence, every day a cheerful voice would call out, 'Good morning!' and I would reply, 'Good morning.' One day I didn't get to the mowing until the afternoon, but when I brought the cuttings to the fence, the same cheerful voice said, 'Good morning!' Puzzled, I climbed up and looked over the fence, and discovered that for the past month I had been in daily conversation with a parrot.

"The joke was on me in more ways than one. Because besides the ridiculously hard work, I was paid a measly $60 a month for a five-day-a-week job. Then one day the lady of the house asked me if I would feed the dogs for an extra $10. Now for me $10 at that time was a fortune. Eva and I were living in a small apartment in Hollywood and we were hoping to have a child, so of course I agreed. But now I had to walk to the dogfood factory the people owned (in addition to a big department store downtown) and cook the dog food. I went up on Rosh Hashanah. I went up on Yom Kippur. And at the end of the month they gave me a measly $7.50—because that month one of the dogs had been sold. That's the kind of people they were. Then one day the lady came and said that the head gardener had quit and she wondered if I would take over his chores as well. 'Yes,' I said, 'but I would need a raise.' 'Oh you refugees!' she shouted. 'You think we're only waiting for you?!'

"So I quit. But thanks to Mrs. Green, a nice woman at the Jewish Employment Service, I started as a helper the very next day at her place, also in Beverly Hills. They had a lemon grove, and the head gardener allowed me to pick some lemons to take home. So I picked a few and stuffed them in my overalls. I had to walk a long way through Beverly Hills to get to the bus station on Sunset Blvd. And the next thing I knew I was stopped by the police, who asked for my identification and threatened to report me to the Greens. I was a legal immigrant but I was still scared of being sent back to Germany. Fortunately, the head gardener told the police the whole story and nothing happened. But these were some of the crazy things I had to put up with in my first days in Los Angeles.

"Later on, of course, after working for the wealthy émigrés and other movie people, things started to turn around. I was able to buy a truck and tools and a power mower and even took on a helper of my own. One of my first, also a refugee, had a thing about clothes. He was an intellectual and always dressed very formally, because he was afraid one of his friends might see him working as a gardener. So he changed clothes when he came to work, and when anybody passed by he hid behind the bushes.

*Rudy the happy gardener*

"Another was Ernest Wolf, the principal of the school in Sweden where Eva and I had worked before coming to the United States. Now I was his boss. But the oddest part was how all us college-educated émigrés, many trained as doctors and lawyers, had been forced out of our careers in Germany and into menial jobs as immigrants in America. But I didn't mind. I loved plants and the out-of-doors. And as an old socialist, I wasn't a snob about manual labor.

"My best and most loyal helper was Jack Opels, a Jewish refugee from Holland, a simple, good-hearted man whom I used to call, with a Dutch pronunciation, 'Fuckah Juckah.' He always came fifteen minutes early, never missed a day. He was also very funny and always came wearing six or seven shirts, because he was terribly afraid of catching a cold. In the morning, he took off the first one, then like the Dance of the Seven Veils, he took off another, and another, and another, and then in the evening he put them all back on again.

"Then there's the time I nearly poisoned the Gershwins..."

*Ira and George Gershwin (1937)*

*Lee and Ira Gershwin (1949) (Photos provided courtesy
Library of Congress Performing Arts Reading Room)*

## CHAPTER 18

# Rhapsody in Red

"**W**hen I want to imagine how royalty must have lived at their height," Rudy continued, "I think about George Gershwin's lyricist brother, Ira, and Ira's wife, Leonore (called Lee), for whom I worked for nine years. It was unbelievable! Servants on top of servants. Cooks and chauffeurs. Swimming pool, tennis court, billiard table, projection room. But the Gershwins were awfully nice to me, they recommended me for a lot of other jobs, and it was through them that I was able to buy our first house.

"When our first son, your brother Thomas, turned two years old, we were still living in the small apartment on Glencoe Way, which in spite of lying in the shadow of the Hollywood Bowl and up the street from Frank Lloyd Wright's Freeman House, was quite cramped, without a yard, and didn't seem the best place to raise a child. Also, I had always dreamed of living on a kibbutz, and when a small chicken ranch in the San Fernando Valley came up for sale, I couldn't resist. But we had no furniture of our own. No refrigerator. No down payment. And the price was $6,000, a fortune in those days. Plus, an émigré friend advised, 'You'll be owing money for eighteen years, and you know what happened in Germany!'

"But the broker kept egging me on. And so did Lee Gershwin, who went with me and her secretary to look at the place, and when we got there, without checking into it, she said, 'Rudy, buy it! How much do you need from Ira?' I said, 'Five hundred dollars?' So Ira gave me 500, as an advance on my salary. And Martin Gang, the prominent Hollywood lawyer, gave me 500. And a rich refugee lady gave me 500. And I had the down payment and then some.

*Rudy basking in the glory of his new house*

"So the Gershwins were not only nice but generous—and very forgiving. My work, besides taking care of the garden, consisted of every Friday bringing some decorative branches for the piano, which the secretary arranged. There wasn't a magnolia tree in Beverly Hills I hadn't robbed for the Gershwins. Then one day driving to work through Benedict Canyon, Fuckah Juckah and I saw that it was aflame with fall color from the wild bushes. So we cut some big branches, which the secretary arranged, and it never looked so beautiful. But when I got home I had a rash, from the wild shrub my horticulture studies hadn't alerted me to—poison oak. The next day Mrs. Gershwin was standing with powdered arms and I said, 'Oh Lee, you also got poison oak!' 'Oh, is that what it is?' she said. 'My Beverly Hills dermatologist didn't know!'

"But it wasn't the end with the Gershwins. And even when Fuckah Juckah fell into the swimming pool with the power mower, they still didn't fire me. Then came the fencing around the tennis court. Like many wealthy people, they wanted the tennis court to be hidden so it was more exclusive, but also, no doubt, so people couldn't see how poorly they played. So I chose some beautiful vines to cover the fencing, but once again my landscaping knowledge fell short—and so did the fencing, which toppled over from the weight of the vines. But again they forgave me. Until one cold winter the bougainvillea I had planted froze. I knew I couldn't start pruning it before the frost was over. So I waited, and Lee waited, and when after I don't know how long I still hadn't cut it—that was the last straw. She came out to hug and kiss me good-bye, stumbled over the steps, and then said, 'Rudy, we have to part.' It was one of my best jobs, so it was a big blow. But I recovered.

"Through Robert Ryan's business manager, I landed him as a customer. Another coup came as a surprise. I was taking care of an empty place that was up for rent. One day a very handsome man introduced himself as the new tenant. He gave me his last name and I asked what his profession was. 'Oh,' he said, 'I'm an actor.' I had never heard of him before. Then he asked me whether I could lower my rate from $17.50 to $12.50 a month. I reluctantly agreed, but he became one of my nicest customers. One day I asked him, 'Why do you call me Mr. Brook? All my other customers call me Rudy.' He said, 'Yes, I'll do that, but under one condition. If you call me Cornel.' And that's how Cornel Wilde behaved all along. [See Appendix N.]

"Then there was Judy Garland, who needed no introduction. And working for her and Vincente Minnelli was the crowning touch

*Robert Ryan in* Odds Against Tomorrow *(1959), Cornel Wilde in* The Perfect Snob *(1941) (both Photofest)*

of my gardening career. Though we did have some glitches along the way. We had started a big landscape job and one day Judy's business manager, a Mr. Singer, sent me a letter saying, 'We will have to discontinue. The financial situation of Mr. and Mrs. Minnelli does not permit continuation.' This was baloney, and both Judy and Vincente ended up suing him for misconduct, and the landscaping job went forward. But besides the work, nobody I know of has ever seen Judy Garland as beautiful as I did!

*Judy Garland (1943) (Public Domain)*

"She was pregnant with Liza at the same time Eva was pregnant with you. They would both end up at Cedars of Lebanon Hospital in East Hollywood (now the sickly blue-painted Scientology Center). One day Judy called me into her dark-green-painted bedroom and there she was, lying in bed with those big white pillows and her big, dark eyes! You saw nothing but the eyes—and a little blouse. And she said, 'Rudy, how I envy you! Your baby boy was born, and I still have to wait for my Caesarian.'"

## CHAPTER 19

# Unholy Trinity

Shortly after Rudy arrived in Los Angeles from New York in December 1939 and moved in with Eva in her apartment on Glencoe Way, Eva became pregnant. The son she bore on September 12, 1940, in Queen of Angels Hospital in Silver Lake (now the Dream Center, run by the Assemblies of God Church), was named Thomas John. Eva had maintained contact with Granach up until Rudy's arrival and had even mentioned this to him in their correspondence, explaining how she'd met the famous actor at Gerda Weinman's clinic, how he'd taken her to some of the high-end salons, and how these had led to the Fritz Lang gardening connection.

She did not mention the affair, but Rudy would have been stupid not to have suspected some hanky-panky, given Eva's Lulu side and Granach's Weimar-era reputation. His jealousy might have been tempered by the nebbishy image Granach presented in *Ninotchka*, which Rudy had gone to see in New York shortly before moving to L.A. But the date of the film's Manhattan opening couldn't have been more portentous—November 9, 1939—the one-year anniversary of the onset of Kristallnacht and just a day before the Bruchs' arrival in America. And it didn't help that Eva had experienced an even more spectacular gala as Granach's personal guest at *Ninotchka*'s world premiere at Grauman's Chinese Theater on October 26, 1939. Grauman's Chinese, so-named for its pagoda-like architecture and now actually owned by a Chinese company, TCL, and renamed the TCL Chinese, was then and remains the Hollywood theater of choice for prestigious premieres. Excitement had been dampened there as well, however, especially for émigrés with loved

*A Grauman's premiere (1920s) (Bison Archives)*

ones caught in the Nazi vise, by Germany's invasion of Poland the previous month, precipitating World War II.

Rudy's most effective distraction from the war and his suspicions about Granach was immersing himself in his work, which he thoroughly enjoyed in every respect: the physical labor, the communion with nature, and the schmoozing with the customers. It also became imperative that he make a go of it, given the prospect of three mouths to feed. Little did he know that the Hollywood connection, which had helped both him and Eva get a foothold in Los Angeles, would prove a double-edged sword in his marriage, now again on the upswing, and for his growing family as well.

Granach didn't drop out of sight after Rudy's arrival, as subsequent events made apparent. But Eva saw him less frequently, partly

*A Nazi parade (1930s) (Alamy)*

due to her renewed married life, partly due to her pregnancy, and also because his post-*Ninotchka* film career, as she'd assumed, had begun to take off—comparatively speaking.

The sexist double standard, which then reigned (and sadly persists) in everyday life and in other fields, was reversed in the movies for foreign actors generally, and German-accented performers specifically. Thus while exotic/erotic female stars such as Marlene Dietrich and Hedy

*Rudy with one of his gardening helpers, Fred Odenheimer, who with his wife, Doro, took in my cousin Michael Meyer upon his immigration to America in 1951.*

Lamarr retained their allure and marquee value in the 1940s, their male counterparts were relegated to minor or supporting roles as foreigners of various stripes—most often Nazis.

Granach himself was frequently cast as a Gestapo official, most notably in *Hangmen Also Die!* (1943), co-written by Bertolt Brecht

*Glamour girls Marlene Dietrich (1936) and Hedy Lamarr (1930s) (both Photofest)*

*Conrad Veidt as the Nazi arch-
villain in* Casablanca *(Photofest)*

*Granach in* Hangmen Also Die! *(frame grab)*

and directed by Fritz Lang. In *The Hitler Gang* (1944) he played the actual Nazi propagandist Julius Streicher, publisher of the virulently anti-Semitic magazine *Der Stürmer* (striker or attacker), who was executed after the Nuremberg Trials and whose despicable legacy lives on in the American neo-Nazi website *The Daily Stormer*. As bitterly ironic as such casting certainly was, it also came, as for Lotte Andor in *Confessions of a Nazi Spy* and *Casablanca*, with the vengeful and practical satisfaction of contributing to the Allied cause. An added boon for Granach, or so he claimed—from additionally playing a Russian in *Ninotchka*, a Pole in *So Ends the Night* (1941), a Greek in *Halfway to Shanghai* (1942), a Spaniard in *For Whom the Bell Tolls* (1943), and an Italian in *Voice in the Wind* (1944)—was that "I became international in Hollywood." As for the real-life part he played with my family, however, he also became a cad.

Any aspersions one might cast on Granach for his ongoing affair with Eva past the point of Rudy's return must extend to her Pandora's box as well. Nor need the actor's several other escapades during this period—to which his cousin, who lived with him, attested—unduly trouble the forgiving of mind. Granach's behavior shortly after Thomas was born, however, according to two of Rudy and Eva's closest friends and fellow Jewish refugees, unequivocally crossed the line.

The aforementioned Trudy Dresdner and Ann "Annchen" (pronounced "UN-shen") Ikenberg had known one or both of my parents in Germany. Trudy they'd met when Rudy joined her husband Richard's opera troupe, the Twenty Jewish Singers, as a concert booker. The Dresdners had found refuge in London before coming to Los Angeles, where Richard became a voice teacher and Trudy did some accounting work and babysitting, including of Tommy. Annchen had been trained as a medical doctor in Germany. She and her husband, Fred, who served briefly as a judge, were like Rudy shut out of their chosen professions during the Nazi period. Also ardent Zionists, they had run into Rudy at Zionist conferences and, like him, intended to emigrate to Palestine.

At first, Annchen recalled, it looked like clear sailing. "The Gestapo officers were sociable and said, 'Oh, I envy you that you can go to California. I wish we could go.' They were not at all so mean, but they had their jobs to do. [And in 1938], certificates were given only to people already in concentration camps. We had all the right connections

*Annchen and Fred Ikenberg (1980s)*
*(courtesy Ruth Splansky)*

and it did us no good!" Except to get Fred out of prison, after his arrested shortly after Kristallnacht, . . ." "because of his key role in Jewish immigration to Palestine," to which—as we learned earlier—the Nazis were then favorably inclined. "The whole immigration to Palestine will stop immediately if my husband is in jail!" Annchen, in desperation, told the Gestapo officers. And after a quick call to headquarters, Fred was released. Still without visas for Palestine but with papers in hand for the United States, the Ikenbergs embarked for New York in January 1939 and settled in Los Angeles, where Annchen found work in private nursing and Fred became an accountant. They renewed contact with the Bruchs through the émigré grapevine and, along with the Dresdners, made Alexander Granach's acquaintance—with disastrous results.

## CHAPTER 20

# Doubting Thomas

The settings of Trudy and Annchen's separate encounters with Granach, around the time of Tommy's birth, differ. The gist of their exchanges, however—Trudy's related to me shortly before, and Annchen's shortly after Rudy's death—is corroborative, and the import equally shocking.

Trudy's account is the following. While having her hair done at a Hollywood beauty salon also frequented by Eva and other émigrés,

*Trudy Dresdner*

she sat admiring a baby photo of Tommy pinned to the wall. Trudy not only knew of the recent birth, but Eva, knowing how much her childless friend loved children, had, as Eva put it, been "sharing my Tommy with her from the very first day he was born (even before)." Then, as Trudy was gushing to the hairdresser about her quasi-godson, Granach entered the salon, apparently hoping to see Eva. Trudy had met the actor through Eva and he'd even helped Richard acquire some voice-train-

ing clients. But however favorable an opinion she may have held of him to that point, it instantly plunged when he strolled over to Trudy, said "*Guten Tag, meine Damen* (Good day, ladies)," pointed to the baby photo and blurted, with matched expression of fatherly pride, "Zat's my son! *Süß, nicht wahr* (Sweet, don't you think)?"

The hairdresser's jaw dropped and Trudy was aghast. "How can you say such a thing?" she demanded. "And in public!"

"*Ach*, you petty bourgeois," Granach said with a shrug.

"What makes you any better?" Trudy shot back.

"I believe in free love."

"Well, this time it comes with a cost—to a loving family, and to you as well!"

Granach started to respond, then simply turned and walked out the door.

Trudy's bravado turned to anguish when she thought of the possible repercussions of Granach's indiscretion.

"I wonder how many others he's told," she whispered to the hairdresser.

"This was the first I've heard."

"Let's keep it that way, all right?" Trudy pleaded, and the hairdresser nodded.

To no avail, according to Annchen, who recalled that Granach "went around to friends of the family," not only repeating his "Zat's my son!" boast but with a copy of Tommy's baby photo in hand! Thus, whether from the adulterer's lips or by word of mouth, before long the scandalous news had made the rounds of the Bruchs' émigré circle and come full circle to Eva and Rudy as well. And, as Trudy and many others had feared, the cost to the Bruch family, and especially to Tommy, was considerable. For as much as Rudy (or anyone) might have wished to dismiss Granach's brazen claim, given Eva's intimate contact with him and with no DNA testing yet available to resolve the matter, there was ample reason, especially at this early stage in the young boy's life, to put his paternity in doubt.

This uncertainty, compounded by Rudy's anger toward Eva—whose affair with Granach the actor's public boasts affirmed—clearly affected his feelings toward Tommy. His relationship with "his" first-born, from all reports, was troubled from the start, and deteriorated further, in a vicious cycle, because of Tommy's unruly behavior—no doubt prompted, at least partly, by Rudy's ambivalence toward him. "Tommy was difficult," "a problem child," "a handful" from a very early age, Trudy, Annchen, and other of my parents' friends recalled,

*Rudy as a child·*　　　　　*Tom as a child (with Eva and me)*

and he began seeing a child psychiatrist at age five. The friends were quick to add that, over time, Tommy's strong physical resemblance to Rudy rather than Granach assuaged their, and Rudy's, qualms—but the die had been cast.

Rudy's initial doubt about Tommy's paternity and the end to all doubt about Eva's adultery may not have been the sole causes for my parents' perpetual shouting matches, which extended into my childhood and lasted throughout their marriage—generally culminating in Rudy's slamming the door as he stormed from the house. Whatever the reason, life in the Brook family was light years from the *Father Knows Best/Leave It to Beaver* sitcoms of the feel-good fifties. Whether Rudy additionally muddied the waters through a revenge fling of his own is unlikely, at least according to family friends who confided in me about the Granach affair after Rudy's death. He was quite charming and occasionally even flirtatious, they averred, but, as far as they knew, he never crossed the line. And while the Granach business surely soured some of his feelings for Eva, Rudy remained to the end, from my perception, still very much in love with his Hebrew school sweetheart.

How then to explain Granach's unconscionable behavior, which not only disrupted a father-son relationship but further destabilized an already rocky marriage? Narcissism and possessiveness, character traits Granach apparently had in abundance, take us only so far. As

*Granach and Martha in 1914
(Akademie der Künste, Granach-
Archiv)*

*Granach and Gad*

do possible anguish over his geographically distant son, Gad, whom
he might never see again, and the outside chance of starting a new
family with Tommy and Eva. A more telling motivation, I believe,
lies in the Ostjude/Westjude conflict, which Granach had overcome
in his acting career but been scarred by in his youth and subjected
to again in his marriage to Martha Guttmann. As Gad, conceived
shortly before Granach was drafted into World War I, explained in his
memoir: "He could never feel too comfortable around my mother's family, who were opposed to the relationship. My father was
an Ostjude, an Eastern European Jew from Galicia. . . . This, for my
grandfather, who considered himself a German Jew through and
through, was not at all appropriate. He condescendingly referred
to my father as the 'Galizianer'"—an epithet for the lowest of the
low among the Ostjuden. Although Martha didn't share her family's extreme prejudice, she inadvertently reinforced Granach's

inferiority complex by helping the untutored Eastern Jew with the then-still bowed legs "become familiar not only with German culture but with culture in general."

Their five-year marriage ended shortly after Granach returned from the war, the rupture precipitated at least partly, he told young Gad, because "your mother is so petit bourgeois." Now jump forward to early World War II Los Angeles, where Granach was now in a position—like the rough-hewn studio moguls vis-à-vis the hoity-toity Westjuden who'd snubbed their kind in Europe—to give the petit bourgeois in his social circle (including my anti-Ostjuden father) "a taste of their own medicine!"

*Rudy's quasi-kibbutz*

## CHAPTER 21

# "Pop Goes the Weasel"

Round and round the mulberry bush
The farmer chased the weasel.
The farmer fell down, and off went his gun—
Pop goes the weasel!
    —lyrics to *All Around the Mulberry Bush* (personal variant)

Curiously enough, Granach's transgression, with long-term traumatic consequences for Tommy, didn't lead to complete ostracizing of the would-be cuckolder from the less prestigious salons my parents participated in and sometimes hosted. Whether two-year-old Tommy's growing resemblance to Rudy caused the rapprochement, Granach was invited in 1942 to speak at a *Gruppe* gathering. The actor's Hollywood celebrity stature no doubt played a part in his guest appearance. "We were snobbish," Annchen recalled, underscoring the Westjuden mindset. "Not everyone was invited to join. You had to be academic and . . . have a professional background. We took turns giving talks. . . . Sometimes we had guest speakers, like Alexander Granach, a movie person."

I can't imagine Rudy's subjecting himself to any of the salons at which Granach appeared. But a drastic change that facilitated at least a partial truce with his archrival was the family's move in 1942 to the chicken farm in Van Nuys, the one that Rudy had managed to purchase, with the Gershwins' and others' help, for a whopping $6,000. The San Fernando Valley was "the sticks" in those days, still a largely agricultural region a long streetcar ride from downtown and other more populated areas. But the Brooks in other ways were less isolated than before, given the many chicken farms that dotted the Valley, most of them owned by fellow refugee Jews, some of whom became close family friends.

Rudy's fulfillment of his "long-standing dream" didn't sit so well with Eva, at least initially. "But once I discovered this charming little Spanish-style cottage, surrounded by a two-acre farm with twenty-three apricot trees, as well as apple, fig, walnut, and orange trees, I changed my attitude!" And she might have added tangerine, plum, and loquat trees, Muscat and Concord grapes, a boysenberry patch, and for me the crowning touch, a mulberry bush—more like a stunted, umbrella-shaped tree, with drooping branches and delicious purple berries. Before feasting ourselves on them, the neighbor kids and I loved to scamper around the mulberry bush, singing the refrain quoted in the epigraph—whose punchline now seems uncannily resonant with what my father no doubt would have liked to do to Granach.

The farm also served as partial therapy for little Tommy, for whom, Eva explained, "the farm animals were a delight. Besides more than a thousand chickens, we also had ducks, rabbits, goats, even a cow named 'Judy' who gave us milk and butter during the war years. And of course a dog and a cat. Our farm became a recreation center for our friends and even strangers, who loved to spend their Sundays and holidays there. One of them said, 'Happiness is having friends who have a farm.' The apricot-picking season was the highlight of it all." As I fondly recall, for not only being allowed but encouraged to climb the trees, fill the buckets, and help hawk the crates of fruit we sold on the street.

Leave it to Granach to put another crimp in the Brooks' comparative bliss. Comparative given the war still raging in the mid-1940s, an anxious time for everyone and no picnic for German-speaking Jews. All German (and Italian) nationals were required to register as enemy aliens, were subject to increased scrutiny by officialdom, and at least in Los Angeles were curfew-bound in their homes from 8 pm to 6 am and warned by police not to speak German in public (though their accents gave them away). Known leftists, such as

Lion Feuchtwanger, and those with whom they'd associated, such as Salka Viertel, found themselves under FBI surveillance. And though in much smaller numbers and for shorter periods than the Japanese, German and Italian immigrants and U.S. citizens were also interned, including a number of Jewish refugees. Jews, overall, faced overt anti-Semitism of astounding proportions. Even after Kristallnacht, in a 1939 poll that matched earlier polls in the decade, 53 percent of Americans said that Jews "were different" and "should be restricted," with 10 percent calling for their outright deportation. By 1941, a majority still said that Jews (making up just 2 percent of the overall population) had "too much power," and by 1945 this figure actually rose to 67 percent! Openly anti-Jewish sentiment wouldn't begin to abate until awareness of the Holocaust became widespread after the war. Though even then, in the early Cold War period, the tendency to lump Jews and Communists together threw their American patriotism into question, and after the establishment of Israel in 1948, charges of dual loyalty (echoing the European stab-in-the-back canard) additionally marred their full acceptance.

Worst of all for the Brooks (who changed their name in 1944 partly to minimize the Teutonic and Jewish aspersions) was the constant foreboding about their relatives and friends in Germany, foreboding that was devastatingly borne out by postwar reports. Eva's comment about the effects of her mother's succumbing to cancer when she was twelve seems a fitting epitaph as well for the cloud the Nazi terror cast on her family's wartime and early postwar existence: "beauty and happiness turned into tragedy and death."

Granach, as indicated earlier, was spared this particular anguish thanks to his closest relatives' foresight in emigrating to America in the 1920s and to Israel shortly before Kristallnacht. Instead, toward war's end in early 1945, he caused another major stir in the Brook family. And though it can't compare, in its devastating effect on Tommy, with his "Zat's my son!" pronouncements, the incident was equally bizarre and an apt climax to this many-layered memoir. I was told three versions of this remarkable story—the first again by

Trudy Dresdner, in confidence, before Rudy's death; the other two by Annchen and Eva herself, both after Rudy's death. My mother's version, recounted in the presence of my wife, Karen, diverged from Trudy's and Annchen's on one important point. But first the background.

Despite Granach's nonstop film work in Hollywood following *Ninotchka*, "his true passion was always live theater," Gad recalled. "His big break on Broadway happened in December 1944, in *A Bell for Adano*" (adapted from the John Hersey novel), in the uncannily ironic role of the fisherman, Tomasino (little Thomas!).

Another "true passion" of Granach's, touted in a 2012 documentary on Granach (more on this in the Epilogue), was for Lotte Lieven—based on their affair in Berlin in the 1920s, two brief encounters in Switzerland in the 1930s, and a long-distance correspondence thereafter. According to both Trudy and Annchen, however, in winter 1945, while still starring as Tomasino on Broadway, Granach contacted Eva and made an astonishing "proposal"—that she drop everything, leave the farm in Van Nuys, come to New York with Tommy, and marry him! And what did Eva do? According to her two close friends, she dropped everything and boarded a train for New York with Tommy, fully intending (after divorcing Rudy) to marry Granach. But alas, somewhere along the then five-day cross-country trip, possibly during a change of trains in Chicago, she learned that on March 14th Granach had collapsed on stage, been rushed to the hospital, and died of an embolism during an appendectomy operation. Shocked and heartbroken but feeling beholden, she continued on with Tommy to New York and attended Granach's funeral.

Eva, also some forty years later, at first denied to Karen and me that anything of the sort had occurred, only relenting after I divulged what Trudy and Annchen had related. Then it all poured out, generally matching her friends' accounts—with one crucial exception. Upon receiving Granach's long-distance proposal, and "after some soul-searching," Eva claimed she decided NOT to accept it. Upon hearing of his sudden death, however, she did board a train to New York, with Tommy, and attended Granach's funeral.

I'll let the reader decide whose version seems more credible. I'll only add that when Eva finally chose to give her side of the story, she prefaced it, face all aglow, with perhaps the most astounding comment of all about her former lover—one I'd never heard her say about Rudy and one I'll never forget—"He was a WONDERFUL man!"

*Mike Odenheimer (left) and me*

*The Odenheimers and me (far left)*

# epilogue

It couldn't have been more than a few weeks after Granach's late March funeral (in the Jewish tradition, held as soon as possible after death occurs) that Eva returned to the West Coast—and resumed intimate relations with Rudy. Indeed, judging by my normal-term birth on February 4, 1946, I can vouch for one of their sexual encounters having occurred sometime in late April or early May 1945 (I like to think May 8th, VE-Day).

I grew up on the Van Nuys farm and—except for the parental tantrums and perpetual feuding between Rudy and Tommy—have mostly idyllic memories: in addition to the apricot harvest, of indulging in the cornucopia of fruit in our veritable Garden of Eden (including a forbidding apple tree outside my bedroom window); of collecting fresh eggs from the hen coops in the morning on my tricycle; of Rudy's taking me on his gardening rounds where I met Peter Lorre, Robert Ryan, and Cornel Wilde; and, last not least, of prancing around and feasting on my very own mulberry bush. When Eva later started teaching kindergarten and Rudy added landscape design to his gardening before eventually becoming a real estate broker, the chickens were sold off and apricot vending ceased. But I still had a two-acre playground and a neighbor my age, Mike Odenheimer (son of the previously mentioned Fred and Doro Odenheimer), to enjoy it with.

My relationship with Tom was another matter. Besides our nearly six-year age difference and few shared interests, I sensed a certain bitterness toward me throughout my childhood and beyond. That this stemmed at least partly from Tom's troubles with Rudy was confirmed after our father's death in 1983, when Tom demanded a larger share of the estate because, as he told the family lawyer—in front of my mother and Karen, just before slamming me with his briefcase—"Vincent was the favored child!"

Clearly more than garden-variety sibling rivalry was behind Tom's violent outburst. But as startling as it was, the acknowledgement of our Jacob and Esau-like relationship was not. The fraternal fissures, and their biblical resonances (thanks to Hebrew school), were ones I had sensed growing up. Despite us both being of German-Jewish descent, we were from the start, like the Ost and Westjuden in historian Steven Aschheim's phrase, "brothers and strangers." After straining to put aside some of our differences during the later stages of our parents' lives, following Eva's death in 1987, we broke off relations completely. In one of our last encounters, I broached the Granach affair with Tom, and was struck by the indifference he expressed toward events that, for him above all, were likely of life-altering consequence. Whether his dismissiveness was sincere I will never know. Interestingly, however, despite or because of his Oedipal issues, Tom ended up following in Rudy's footsteps and even doing him one better, by passing the California bar and actually practicing law for several years, before also going into real estate.

For me, the Granach affair offered at least a partial explanation for Tom's and my parents' troubles. But I had little cause to dwell on the role it played until German filmmaker Angelika Wittlich, having learned of the affair through a family acquaintance, interviewed me at length for her 2012 documentary for German television, *Alexander Granach: Da geht ein Mensch (Alexander Granach: There Goes a Mensch).* The title, a nod to Granach's autobiography, was, at least for me, rich in irony, given that "Mensch," in German, simply means "person," but in Yiddish, "a very decent human being."

The backdrop for the interview, the Villa Aurora (now funded and run by the German Federal Foreign Office and the Federal Government Commissioner for Culture and the Media), also couldn't have been more à propos—for Wittlich and for me. For her, besides its iconic Southern California beauty, the Villa had been the New Weimar residence of Granach's savior, Lion Feuchtwanger (until his death in 1958), and his salonnière wife, Marta (until her death

in 1987). For me, and for Eva's relations with Granach, the Villa lay directly below the beautiful modernist house my parents had built following the sale of their Van Nuys property at a considerable profit in 1963, and where they lived out their roller-coaster lives.

Imagine, then, my utter shock and dismay, upon viewing the DVD Wittlich sent me in advance of a private screening at the Villa, that my entire lengthy interview had ended up on the cutting room floor! Wittlich's excuse, that Eva's story "didn't

*DVD cover for the Granach film (Zorro Filmverleih)*

fit into the larger narrative," itself told only half the story. The reason it didn't fit was because it clashed jarringly and irretrievably with the fairytale Wittlich eventually concocted, of the "true love" between notorious womanizer Granach and Lotte Lieven, based on a short affair, sporadic encounters, and a correspondence with gaping omissions. Besides ignoring Granach's affair with and proposal to my mother, the film failed to mention his "great love," the one he "really never got over"—Elisabeth Bergner! So much for documentaries as the last bastion of truth—always an unattainable goal but at least one worth striving for. The best way to describe my reaction to Wittlich's "mockumentary" is to paraphrase Eva's reaction to her having to wear the dresses, made for her by her mother, that were blackened after her death: It was like burying the truth all over again.

*Portraits by Eva created in the 1980s at the artists workshop in San Miguel de Allende, Mexico*

I expressed my extreme displeasure with the film to Wittlich personally, and I did not attend the Villa screening. Viewing the film in public only would have added to my resentment and frustration, and voicing my objections, just prior to the film's airing on German television, would have served no useful purpose. The desire to finally set the record straight in this memoir, however, was certainly one motivation for writing it. More importantly, I felt that this part tragic/part redemptive story of Nazi victims, combined with Hollywood's part beneficial/part baleful role in the tale, and the conflict between Ost and Westjuden it underscored, added a unique, micro-historical wrinkle to those uncommonly turbulent times.

As to whether I have dishonored my mother's memory by airing her adultery in public, I can only say that my learning of the affair with Granach did not undermine my affection for her, then or now. It actually made her a more interesting person to me, and to others who knew her and with whom I've shared the family secret. The woman we all knew as a devoted kindergarten teacher and gifted portraitist but also as rather shy and a bit naïve, turned out to be far more adventurous and worldly than we'd imagined.

My sympathy for my father, meanwhile, has only grown with the clue the Granach affair provides for what underlay much of his problems with Eva and Tom. This is not to absolve Rudy of all guilt in the matter. The slight to his manhood and resentment toward Eva notwithstanding, suspecting that young Tommy might not be his biological son does not ethically justify his having withheld fatherly affection from him. Nevertheless, I cherish the love of nature and strong social conscience my father passed on to both Tom and me, and which I highlighted in the section on Rudy's gardening and his work with Hechalutz. While he was clearly proud of the part he played in saving thousands of Jewish lives, he never, as far as I know, sought recognition for it. I also greatly respect his acting on his humanitarian principles to the end, which included, after retirement, volunteering with Amnesty International and helping enforce fair-housing laws.

Perhaps most of all, writing this memoir has reinforced my admiration—begun much too late in life—for the extreme hardships my parents experienced and the many sacrifices they made. In surmounting the traumatic break with their homeland, the tragic loss of relatives and friends in the Holocaust, and the challenge of starting life anew in a distant land, Rudy and Eva—along with a legion of émigrés who suffered through the Nazi period—displayed a courage, resourcefulness, and perseverance that qualify as heroic by any measure. The obstacles they overcame certainly dwarf any I've had to face, thanks to the postwar period in which I was born and the life of comparative comfort, security, and privilege my parents made possible.

As for my brother, as I mentioned, the memoir's rehashing of Eva's relationship with Granach, his proposing to her shortly before his death, and her possible acceptance, would not be news to him. I naturally feel sympathy for Tom's plight due to the Granach affair and its repercussions, the full brunt of which I thankfully was spared.

*The Brook family in their Van Nuys home, late 1940s.*

The fallout obviously weighed most heavily on him in the short term and caused him the most longterm anguish, and for that I'm profoundly saddened.

As for Alexander Granach, I have tried to avoid presenting him monochromatically as the arch villain of the piece. Not to dismiss his disturbing (if not disturbed) behavior, I have sought to place it in personal psychological and broader social context. Granach, like the rest of us, was many things—in his case, a prodigiously talented actor demoted from stardom in Germany to playing second fiddle in Hollywood, a deeply insecure little man despite his comparative celebrity and sexual conquests, and a one-time Communist Ostjude from a poor peasant background itching to get even with Westjuden high hats and the petit bourgeoisie. Fortunately, at least for me, Granach's ultimate revenge fantasy, of marrying Eva and getting "little Thomas" in the bargain, remained just that.

# timelines & appendices

# timelines

### ALEXANDER GRANACH

**1890**  Born Jessaya Granach in Werbiwci, Galicia, to a poor farmer's family

**1896–1903**  Works as a baker's helper in the family business in Horodenka

**1904**  Moves on his own to Stanislau after his first heartbreak with Riffkele, has his first romantic relationship with Malka

**1906**  Moves to Lemberg (Lviv), discovers theater

**1912**  Moves to Berlin to work in theater

**1914**  Signs a five-year contract with Max Reinhardt's company, marries Martha Guttmann

**1915**  Conceives son Gad before going to war

**1919**  Returns to Germany, meets four-year-old Gad, divorces Martha, continues working with Reinhardt, becomes involved with leftist politics

**1921**  First major stage success as Shylock in *The Merchant of Venice*

**1922**  Begins film career as Knock in *Nosferatu*

**1923**  Stars in *Schatten—Eine nächtliche Halluzination* (*Shadows: A Nocturnal Hallucination*)

**Mid-to-late 1920s**  Becomes a theatrical superstar ("King of the Eastern Jews"), has an affair with Lotte Lieven, among others

**1931**  Stars in *Kameradschaft*, co-stars as Marat in *Danton*

**1933**  Flees Germany for Switzerland, renews relations with Lotte Lieven

**1934**  Starts a Yiddish theater group in Warsaw, stages the anti-Nazi play *The Yellow Patch*

**1935**  Starts a Yiddish theater company in Kiev

**1936**  Makes two Russian films: the anti-Nazi *The Fight* and pro-Romani *Gypsies*

**1936**  Caught in Stalin's Great Purge, imprisoned as a "persona non grata"

**1938**  Through Lion Feuchtwanger's intercession, leaves the USSR, emigrates to the United States

**1939**  Starts an affair with Eva, is cast in *Ninotchka*

**1940**  Claims he fathered Eva's newborn son, Tommy

**1942**  Appears at *Gruppe* salons, whose members include Eva and Rudy

**1943**  Plays a Gestapo official in *Hangmen Also Die!*

**1944**  Plays actual Nazi propagandist Julius Streicher in *The Hitler Gang*

**1944**  Plays a concentration camp inmate in *The Seventh Cross*

**1944**  Stars as Tomasino on Broadway in *A Bell for Adano*

**1945**  Asks Eva to come to New York with Tommy and marry him

**1945**  Collapses on stage and dies of an embolism during an appendectomy operation

# RUDOLF (RUDY) BRUCH/BROOK

**1904** Born in Magdeburg, Germany, to Elise Szkolny Bruch and Oscar Bruch, a successful wholesale yardage salesman

**1915** Falls in love with Eva in Hebrew School

**Mid-1920s** Moves to Berlin to study law

**1929** Meets Eva again, strikes up a romance

**1931** Marries Eva in a Jewish wedding

**1933** Passes the Bar but can't practice law because of the Nazis' anti-Jewish laws

**1933** Works as a booking agent for the Twenty Jewish Singers

**1934** Does clerical work at Gertrud Feiertag's Jewish children's school in Caputh, near Berlin, where Eva is a full-time teacher

**1934–1938** Works for Hechalutz in Berlin, arranging marriages enabling Jews to immigrate to Palestine

**1935** Arrested for "impertinence" toward the Nazi authorities

**1937** Visits Palestine and sees the mixed results of his marriage brokering

**1937** Separation #1: Rudy, with Eva left behind in Germany, moves to Västraby, Sweden, a hoped-for stopover on the way to Palestine

**1938** His father, Oscar, dies of natural causes

**1938** Reunion #1: Eva rejoins Rudy in Sweden, where they both work at a Jewish school before emigrating to America

**1938** Rudy and Eva meet her sister, Ilse, and Ilse's husband, Karl Meyer, in Lund, Sweden, as a farewell and to witness young Peter Meyer's baptism

**1938** Rudy and Eva arrive in New York on the second day of Kristallnacht

**1938–1939** Separation #2: While Eva goes to Hollywood to work as a masseuse, Rudy stays in New York, gets help from a refugee friend, Lotte Andor, takes horticulture classes, works as a gardener

**1939** Reunion #2: Rudy rejoins Eva in Hollywood, gets gardening jobs with prominent European refugees and Hollywood big-wigs

**1940** Thomas John Brook (formerly Bruch) is born to Eva and (possibly) Rudy—the paternity initially in doubt because of Granach

**1942** Rudy's mother, Elise, and sister, Margot, die in a Polish transit camp

**1942** With help from Lee Gershwin and her husband, Ira, Rudy buys a chicken farm in the San Fernando Valley

**1943** Eva's father, Hans Eger, perishes in Theresienstadt, and Gertrud Feiertag is gassed at Auschwitz

**1944** Rudy officially changes the family name from Bruch to Brook

**1946** Son Vincent is born

**1950s** Rudy sells the chickens, goes into landscape gardening, and eventually becomes a real estate broker

**1963** He sells the Valley property, builds a new house in Pacific Palisades, directly above the Feuchtwanger's Villa Aurora

**1960s–1980s** He gradually retires from real estate, becomes active in the community, does volunteer work for fair housing and Amnesty International

**1983** Dies of stomach cancer

## EVA EGER BRUCH/BROOK

**1906** Born in Magdeburg, Germany, to Alma Blumenthal Eger and Hans Eger, who owns a small pharmacy

**1915** Meets Rudy in Hebrew School

**1915** Alma is diagnosed with breast cancer, has a mastectomy

**1918** Alma dies

**1919** Eva drops out of high school, attends a women's trade school, then art school

**1926** Moves to Berlin, studies gymnastics

**1928** Gets a public school job teaching drawing and gymnastics

**1929** Meets Rudy and their romance begins, gets a teaching job at Gertrud Feiertag's school on the Frisian island of Norderney

**1931** Marries Rudy in a Jewish wedding

**1931** Moves with Feiertag to her school in Caputh

**1933** Supports herself and Rudy due to his proscription from practicing law

**1937** Separation #1: Stays in Germany while Rudy moves to Sweden, en route (he hopes) to Palestine

**1938** Reunion #1: Rejoins Rudy in Sweden when he agrees to go to America instead, witnesses Peter Meyer's baptism in Lund and bids farewell to her sister, Ilse, and Ilse's husband, Karl.

**1938** Eva and Rudy arrive in New York on the second day of Kristallnacht

**1938–1939** Separation #2: Eva goes to Hollywood to work as a masseuse, starts an affair with Granach, while Rudy stays in New York

**1939** Reunion #2: She asks Rudy to rejoin her in Los Angeles

**1940** Son Thomas John is born (but who's the father?)

**1942** Rudy's mother, Elise, and sister, Margot, perish in a Polish transit camp

**1942** Eva moves with Rudy and Tommy into the newly purchased Valley chicken farm

**1943** Her father, Hans, dies in Theresienstadt, and Gertrud Feiertag is gassed at Auschwitz

**1945** Granach dies (before Eva can marry him?)

**1946** Her and Rudy's second son, Vincent, is born

**Late 1940s** Takes education classes

**1950–1970s** Works as a kindergarten teacher in the West Valley

**1980s** After Rudy dies in 1983, she retires from teaching, keeps busy with drawing and other artwork

**1987** Dies of heart failure

# appendix a

## ERNST LUBITSCH AND BILLY WILDER

*Lubitsch (left, with Maurice Chavalier); Wilder (right, with Gloria Swanson) (Bison Archives and Alamy)*

A COMEDY STAR in Germany in the 1910s playing pointedly Jewish types, Ernst Lubitsch (1892–1947) shifted by the late 1910s to directing light comedies and historical dramas. The success of the latter caught Hollywood's eye and, lured by the resources of the movie capital, he came to Los Angeles in 1922. Working first with superstar Mary Pickford, next with the fledgling Warner Bros., and eventually with Paramount and MGM, he tilted toward the genre that would become his lasting legacy and immortalize "the Lubitsch touch": sophisticated comedies, often set in Europe. Expanding into musicals in the early sound era, he was hailed as a master of the new form and in 1935, unprecedentedly for a director, was appointed head of production at Paramount. With *Ninotchka*, and the chance to work with Greta Garbo, he moved back to MGM, where he would also make the classic *The Shop Around the Corner* (1940), set in Budapest, Hungary. Before health problems curtailed his output in the mid-1940s, he managed to make one of his most enduring and, after the Holocaust, controversial masterpieces, the anti-Nazi satirical comedy *To Be or Not to Be* (1942).

The Galician-born and Vienna-raised Billy Wilder (1906–2002) moved to Berlin during the Weimar period. Working first as a journalist and occasional taxi-dancer (gigolo), he turned to screenwriting in the late 1920s, then joined the exodus of Jewish film personnel following Hitler's rise. He directed his first film in Paris in 1934 and made the leap to Hollywood the same year. Initially working strictly as a screenwriter, such as on *Ninotchka*, he became one of Hollywood's first writer-directors with the screwball comedy *The Major and the Minor* (1942), and reached the pinnacle of the ranks with his Oscar-winning (Best Picture, Director, and Screenwriter) *The Lost Weekend* (1945), about the effects of alcoholism. A hard edge, biting humor, and genre flexibility marked his body of work, whose subsequent classics ranged from problem films such as *The Lost Weekend* to film noir (*Double Indemnity*, 1944; *Sunset Blvd.*, 1950; *Ace in the Hole*, 1951; *Witness for the Prosecution*, 1957), social satires (*A Foreign Affair*, 1948; *Stalag 17*, 1953; *The Apartment*, 1960), and sex farces (The *Seven Year Itch*, 1955; *Some Like It Hot*, 1959; *Irma La Deuce*, 1963).

# appendix b

## MAX REINHARDT AND THE EXPRESSIONIST MOVEMENT

*Max Reinhardt (1911) and Expressionist cinema* (The Cabinet of Dr. Caligari, *1920) (1: George Grantham Bain Collection, Library of Congress; 2: Photofest)*

THE Austrian-Jewish Max Reinhardt (1873–1943) was hands down the German-speaking world's, if not all Europe's, most successful and influential theater director/impresario from the first decade of the 1900s through the Weimar period. Historian Lotte Eisner called him "the Kaiser of the Berlin theater." Reinhardt also had immense impact on Weimar cinema by virtue of the many prominent creative figures who, like Granach, moved fluidly between the stage and motion pictures. Ernst Lubitsch got his start as an actor with Reinhardt, as did future Granach director F. W. Murnau, and noted film noir director Edgar G. Ulmer began as Reinhardt's, and later Murnau's, set designer. Reinhardt toured the United States with *The Miracle* in 1924 and *A Midsummer Night's Dream* in 1927, and by 1930 ran eleven stages in Berlin, from the intimate to the grandiose. While maintaining a residence in Germany, he reprised *A Midsummer Night's Dream* at the Hollywood Bowl in 1934 and adapted it to the Hollywood screen in 1935 with a cast including James Cagney, Olivia de Havilland, and Mickey Rooney. The Nazis, however, who had begun banning American films with Jewish actors and banished all Jewish personnel from Hollywood-branch studios in Germany, banned Reinhardt's *A Midsummer Night's Dream* because of his Jewish ancestry and that of Felix Mendelssohn, whose music was used in the film. Finally, following Germany's annexation of Austria in 1938, Reinhardt had had enough. He emigrated to America by way of Great Britain, opened a theater school in Hollywood, and produced and directed plays on Broadway until his death in 1943. Max's German-born son, Gottfried Reinhardt, became an assistant director to Lubitsch in Hollywood and a consort of Salka Viertel's. Gottfried also worked on an early script (as did Viertel) for *Ninotchka,* and produced Garbo's last film, *Two-Faced Woman* (1941).

The German Expressionist movement lasted roughly from the early 1900s through the mid-1920s. Inspired by Post-Impressionist painters such as van Gogh and Munch, and the aesthetic principles of the Cubists and Fauves, Expressionism sought to represent internal rather than surface reality and affected all the arts.

Expressionist theater, specifically, with which Reinhardt was closely associated, rebelled against the prevailing realist and naturalist schools and came to dominate the German stage from the 1910s through the early 1920s. Favoring gestural acting and masks, as well as distorted set design, costuming, and makeup, Expressionist plays probed psychological states and social problems. Key playwrights and impresarios, besides Reinhardt and those mentioned in the body of the text, were the Jewish Walter Hasenclever, Leopold Jessner, and Jürgen Fehling. The style eventually influenced cinema as well, first and foremost the Frankenstein-inspired horror film *The Cabinet of Dr. Caligari* (1920), as well as the first major vampire film, *Nosferatu* (1922), co-starring Granach. Fritz Lang's futurist drama *Metropolis* (1927) was one of the last German Expressionist films.

# appendix c

## HELENE WEIGEL AND ELISABETH BERGNER

*Helene Weigel (1966) and Elisabeth Bergner (1935) (1: Photo Hans Joachim Sprengberg/ DLA-Marbach; 2: Public Domain)*

THE Vienna-born Jewish actress Helene Weigel (1900–1971) appeared briefly in three Weimar-era films, including Fritz Lang's *Metropolis* (1927) and the Bertolt Brecht-written leftist polemic *Kuhle Wampe, oder: Wem Gehört die Welt* (*Kuhle Wampe, or Who Owns the World*, 1932). She was noted primarily for her stage work, especially as the eponymous Mother Courage and other lead roles in plays by Brecht, whom she married in 1930. Burdened under the Nazis by her Jewishness and both her and Brecht's Communist leanings, the couple fled Germany in 1933. After peripatetic wanderings through Scandinavia and the Soviet Union (where they met the similarly exiled Granach), the couple moved to Los Angeles in 1941. Weigel's German accent limited her theater work in the U.S., and though Brecht co-wrote Lang's anti-Nazi *Hangmen Also Die!* (1943), neither of them felt comfortable in Hollywood or materialistic American society. After Brecht's run-in with the House Committee on UnAmerican Activities (HUAC) in 1947, the pair returned to Europe and eventually settled in East Germany. In the Soviet-controlled sector and later Soviet-satellite nation, Weigel and Brecht, rather than suspected as security risks, were celebrated as cultural icons. In East Berlin, Brecht established the Berliner Ensemble, a theater that once again allowed Weigel to shine, and of which she became the director after Brecht's death in 1956.

There is no contesting Elisabeth Bergner's (1897–1986) womanly allure, but an additional factor that helps explain Alexander Granach's exceptionally strong attachment to the actress is her place of origin. She was a fellow Galicianer, born in the Ukrainian portion of the province and therefore, unlike my mother and Lotte Lieven, an Ostjude. But as significant as Granach's "great love" for Bergner, her client relationship with my father, and her inspiration for the film *All About Eve* are to this memoir, there is of course much more to be said about the noted actress— and Granach is once again in the picture. Bergner got her first big career break in 1922 when, according to Granach's son, Gad, his then already-famous father chose her to co-star with him in the Berlin production of the ironically titled play (given Granach's reputation), *Der lasterhafte Herr Tschu* (*The Licentious Mr. Chu*). This led to

Bergner's first film role, in *Der Evangeligmann* (*The Evangelist*, 1923), though subsequently in the Weimar era, like Granach, she performed, and shone, mainly on the stage. Seeing the Nazi writing on the wall, Bergner left Germany before Hitler came to power, settling in England with her eventual husband, Hungarian-Jewish stage and film director Paul Czinner. In London she starred in Margaret Kennedy's play *Escape Me Never* in 1934, reprised the role on Broadway, and was nominated for a Best Actress Academy Award for her performance in the 1935 British film adaptation, directed by Czinner. She appeared in 1936 opposite Laurence Olivier in *As You Like It*, the first sound-film version of Shakespeare's play, and the same year starred in J. M. Barrie's last play, *The Boy David*, which he'd written especially for her. In 1943, while starring on Broadway in *The Two Mrs. Carrolls*, Bergner had the *All About Eve*-like experience described in the Prologue. Unlike Helene Weigel, Bergner returned to West rather than East Germany after the war, appearing on stage and screen, most notably for the latter in the Oscar-nominated Best Foreign Language Film, *Der Fussgänger* (*The Pedestrian*, 1974). In 1980 Austria honored her with the Cross of Merit for Science and Art.

# appendix d

## ERWIN PISCATOR AND BERTOLT BRECHT

*Erwin Piscator and Bertolt Brecht (1: Erwin-Piscator-Archiv; 2: Bundesarchiv)*

GERMAN playwrights and theater producers Erwin Piscator (1893–1966) and Bertolt Brecht (1898–1956) both rose to prominence in the Weimar era, escaped Nazi Germany for the Soviet Union, and eventually landed in the United States before returning to their divided postwar homeland. Brecht's involvement with German cinema, besides the aforementioned *Kuhle Wampe*, starring his wife, Helene Weigel, included, most famously, *Die Dreigroschenoper* (*The Three Penny Opea*, 1931), based on his "play with music" (the latter composed by Kurt Weil). Brecht and Piscator were also the major theorists and exponents of "epic theater." Coined by Piscator, epic theater derived from Richard Wagner's notion of the *Gesamtkunstwerk* ("total artwork") and by the Soviet formalist and agitprop (agitation-propaganda) literary and theater movements of the 1920s. Gesamtkunstwerk proposed combining elements of all the arts, formalism emphasized radically innovative technique, while agitprop, as its name suggests, was proudly political and propagandistic. Brecht's distinctive contribution to epic theater was the notion of *Verfremdung* ("alienation" or "estrangement"). Not to be confused with the psychological or sociological concepts, alienation in the epic theater context referred to techniques such as didactic commentary, the mixing of genres, breaking the fourth wall, and incorporating multi-media. All these devices, besides making for a lively theater experience, were mainly designed to prod the audience to engage with the material intellectually, not merely emotionally, and to reflect on process and systems—in the art work and society at large. In America, Piscator led a prominent theater workshop at The New School in New York City, while Brecht, as mentioned earlier, tried his hand at Hollywood, co-writing Lang's *Hangmen Also Die!* Cold War anti-Communism struck Brecht hardest, inducing him, after his HUAC testimony in 1947, to flee again, this time to East Berlin with Helene Weigel. Piscator withstood the Communist witch hunt until 1951, when he decamped to West Berlin. Defying the adage that a prophet has no honor in his own country (albeit one by then bifurcated into Western and Eastern sectors), Brecht established the Berliner Ensemble with Weigel, and Piscator was appointed managing director of the *Freie Volksbuhne* (Free People's Theater).

# appendix e

## CITY SYMPHONIES

*Poster for* Berlin: Symphony of a Metropolis *(Photofest)*

AN OFFSHOOT of the avant-garde cinema movement of the 1920s, the so-called "city symphony" became a prominent if short-lived subgenre of documentary film in the post-World War I period. Responding ambivalently to the vibrancy and excitement but also alienation and disruption of the modern metropolis, and appealing to avant-garde artists in various fields, this new nonfiction form retroactively took its name from *Berlin: Die Sinfonie der Großstadt* (1927, variously translated as *Berlin: Symphony of a Metropolis* or *Berlin: Symphony of a Great City*). Directed by Walter Ruttmann, whose career began in advertising and who "stayed behind" to make films for the Nazis, *Berlin* packs months of wide-ranging activity into a seemingly single bustling day in the life of the German capital. The single-day conceit had become a staple of the city symphony by the time Ruttmann extended it to feature-length format and mainstream move-house exhibition, unlike earlier examples that had been short films shown mainly in "cine clubs." These cafes devoted to non-commercial cinema sprang up first in Paris and quickly spread across Europe, but the city symphony cycle actually began in the United States, with *Manhatta* (1921, about New York City, the title taken from Walt Whitman's poem *Mannahatta*), by American photographer Paul Strand and painter Charles Sheeler. The trend reached its zenith in the late 1920s, highlighted by *Berlin* and other subsequent classics such as *Rien que les heures* (*Nothing But Time*, 1927, about Paris), by Brazilian Alberto Cavalcanti, and *Regen* (*Rain*, 1929, about Amsterdam), by Dutchman Joris Ivens. By decade's end, the city symphony, like most genres, had become ripe for revision and eventual satirizing. Ukrainian director Dziga Vertov's *Man with a Movie Camera* (1929) composited footage from four unidentified Soviet cities and, unlike *Berlin* and company, used them to showcase the wonders of cinema rather than the other way around. Frenchman Jean Vigo's *À propos de Nice* (1931) foregrounded the famed resort town but mainly to mock its sunlit splendor for masking a yawning class divide between well-to-do tourists and the working-class poor who serviced them.

# appendix f

## G. W. PABST AND LOUISE BROOKS

*Director G. W. Pabst (1949) and Louise
Brooks as Lulu (Alamy)*

AUSTRIAN filmmaker Georg Wilhelm (G. W.) Pabst (1885–1967) came to the fore in the Weimar period in Berlin as a director of dark-themed, darkly shot, so-called "street films" (dealing with the seductions and dangers of inner city life), a prototype for what the French later termed *"film noir"* (meaning "black film"). One of his first films, *Die freudlose Gasse (Joyless Street*, 1925), as mentioned in Chapter 2, featured Greta Garbo and paved the way for her eventual superstardom. Besides Garbo, Pabst is credited with discovering or fostering the acting careers of the German Brigitte Helm and Leni Riefenstahl, Danish Asta Nielson, French Lili Damita, and American Louise Brooks. After making two controversial, sexually tinged films with Brooks, *Die Büchse der Pandora (Pandora's Box,* 1929) and *Tagebuch einer Verlorenen (Diary of a Lost Girl,* 1929), Pabst furthered his artistic reputation with a trilogy of early, leftist-leaning sound films: *Westfront* (1930), the aforementioned [in Appendix D] *Die Dreigroschenoper* (1931), and *Kameradschaft* (1931), co-starring Granach. Pabst's attempt to flee Nazi Germany was aborted when he was captured in France in 1938. Although he ended up making two films for the Third Reich, *Komödianten (The Comedians,* 1941) and *Paracelsus* (1944), he gained revenge, if not quite absolution, with *Der letzte Akt (The Last Ten Days,* 1955), remarkably the first postwar feature film dealing critically with Adolf Hitler.

Kansas-born dancer and actor Louise Brooks (1906–1985) joined the cutting-edge Denishawn modern dance company in Los Angeles in 1922 at age 16, and became a featured dancer with the Ziegfeld Follies on Broadway three years later. She began working in film in 1926 and catapulted to Hollywood fame, along with Clara Bow and Colleen Moore, as a "flapper"—the short-skirted, bob-haired, free-spirited female symbol of the Roaring Twenties. Her cultural capital rose and femme fatale persona congealed when Pabst chose her for the Lulu role in *Pandora's Box* (1929), adapted from two Lulu-based expressionist plays by Frank Wedekind. Brooks also starred in Pabst's *Diary of a Lost Girl* (1929) and Italian director Augusto Genina's *Miss Europe* (1930). But the Lulu persona, nurtured by Brooks herself through her well-publicized lesbian affairs, attached itself to the actress to the point of no return—literally, in her inability to regain her leading lady stature in the U.S. In her memoir *Lulu in Hollywood* (1982), Brooks explained her informal "blacklisting" as stemming from her disdain for Hollywood. Biographer Barry Paris put a different spin on her downward spiral, suggesting that her failure to play by Hollywood rules was the chief reason for her relegation to B westerns by the late 1930s and her retirement from the movies thereafter. Brooks was rediscovered by film historians in the revisionist 1950s. Compared favorably to the likes of Greta Garbo and Marlene Dietrich as an icon of cinema's golden age, Henri Langlois, founder of the *Cinémathèque Française*, went further, declaring in 1953: "There is no Garbo! There is no Dietrich! There is only Louise Brooks!"

# appendix g

*HAGANAH*

*Haganah fighters (Palmach Archive)*

SEVERAL small Jewish paramilitary units emerged during the so-called Second Aliyah (second emigration) to then Turkish-controlled Palestine from 1904–1914. After the British Mandate for Palestine established by the 1917 Balfour Declaration, forerunners of *Haganah* (the Defense) were formed within the British army stationed in Palestine. It would become the main Jewish military force in the region after the riots of 1920 (called either the Arab riots or the *Nebi Musa* riots, the latter name referring to a Muslim festival during which the violence erupted). Initially loosely organized and poorly armed, Haganah grew significantly in size and cohesiveness after further riots in 1929 (called either the 1929 Massacres or the *Buraq* [lightning] Uprising) and extended conflict from 1936 to 1939 (called the Arab Revolt or the Great Revolt). Already in 1931, in reaction to Haganah's policy of *havlagah* (restraint), a more militant offshoot, known as the *Irgun* (National Military Organization in the Land of Israel) was formed. Together with its own even more radical offshoot, *Lehi* (Fighters for the Freedom of Israel, aka the Stern Gang), Irgun regularly engaged in terrorist operations including bombings and assassinations. But it was Haganah, in response to the 1939 British White Paper restricting Jewish immigration to Palestine, that perpetrated the most tragically violent pre-Independence act in the Patria disaster. The carnage resulted from a bomb set by Haganah and intended to disable the *SS Patria* ocean liner deporting 1800 Jews from Palestine, but which accidentally killed 267 and injured 172. Friction between Haganah and Irgun escalated in 1944 after the assassination of Lord Moyne, British Minister of State for the Middle East. Carried out by Lehi, the incident led Haganah, through its elite *Palmach* (strike force) unit and in conjunction with the British, to begin kidnapping and deporting members of Irgun. After World War II, Haganah, Irgun, and Lehi joined in forming, however precariously, the Jewish Resistance Movement aimed at driving the British from Palestine. In 1947, under the leadership of David Ben Gurion (later to become the first Israeli Prime Minister), Haganah transformed from a paramilitary force into a full-fledged army. Despite Ben Gurion's lingering doubts about Haganah's preparedness, it held its own in the conflict that followed British withdrawal and the partition of Palestine into Israeli and Arab sectors in 1947. Tom Tugend, along with other volunteers from other countries, was among the Haganah forces that helped Israel emerge victorious in the Arab-Israeli War of 1948–1949 (also called Israel's War of Independence), during which Haganah joined, and was eventually absorbed into, the newly formed Israeli Defense Forces (IDF).

# appendix h

## PERSECUTION OF HOMOSEXUALS IN THE THIRD REICH

*A detail photo from a 2018 revival of the play* Bent *(Martin Sherman, 1979), about the persecution of gays in Nazi Germany. (Photo: Alisabeth Von Presley/Theatre Cedar Rapids, 2018)*

JEWS were clearly the prime target of the Nazis and ultimately suffered by far the largest number of deaths in the Holocaust. But other groups deemed a threat to the regime—Communists, socialists, and those regarded as non-Aryan or otherwise "deviant," such as Romanis, the physically or mentally disabled, and gays—also were persecuted, incarcerated, and murdered en masse. Given women's already subservient position in Germany (as in most countries) and greater acceptance of female intimacy, lesbians generally avoided the harsh treatment of gay men. Male homosexuals, however, who had reached new levels of visibility, acceptance, and even esteem during the Weimar period, as highlighted in the Broadway play and Oscar-nominated film *Cabaret* (1972), were especially stigmatized once Hitler came to power. The Nazis resumed rigorous enforcement of anti-homosexual laws under Paragraph 175, a provision of the German Criminal Code since 1871. Moreover, just as Jews were forced to wear yellow stars of David as symbols of their ethnicity, gay men, once they were sent to the death camps, were made to wear pink triangles as symbols of their sexual orientation. The 1979 Tony-nominated play *Bent* ("bent" being a European epithet for homosexual) by Martin Sherman, a gay American Jew, shed long-overdue light on the previousy little known history of Nazi gay persecution. Nor did Germany's defeat in World War II put an end to discrimination against gays, there or elsewhere. Paragraph 175 remained on the books until 1994, and, to America's even greater shame, homosexuality wasn't fully decriminalized until 2003 (in the Supreme Court's 6–3 decision in *Lawrence v. Texas*), the right to same-sex marriage wasn't affirmed until 2015 (in the court's even more precarious 5–4 decision in *Obergefell v. Hodges*), and employment and workplace discrimination against LGBTQs wasn't outlawed nationwide until 2020 (thanks to the 6–3 decision in *Boystock v. Clayton County*).

# appendix i

## HOLLYWOOD AND HITLER

Confessions of a
Nazi Spy *(1939),*
*Hollywood's first*
*openly anti-Nazi*
*film*

HOLLYWOOD'S reluctance to openly confront Hitler and Nazism during the 1930s has long troubled and perplexed historians and the ethically minded, all the more so given the largely Jewish-dominated movie industry at the time. The importance of the German and overall European market to the American studios' bottom line seems scant justification for the moguls not only turning a blind eye to the Nazis' anti-Jewish rhetoric and policies—which included the removal of all Jewish personnel from their branches in Germany—but also for their giving Hitler a say in the content of Hollywood films. Not until 2013, however, with the near simultaneous publication of Ben Urwand's *The Collaboration: Hollywood's Pact with Hitler* and Thomas Doherty's *Hollywood and Hitler: 1933–1939*, would this controversial topic be rigorously revisited—and exacerbated—by Urwand's incendiary claim that all the major studios engaged in outright complicity with the Nazi regime. Doherty offered a more measured account, emphasizing that only MGM, Paramount, and non-Jewish-headed Twentieth Century Fox had caved to Hitler's ultimatums, while Warner Bros., besides removing its operations from Germany rather than giving in to the Führer, had helped found the Hollywood Anti-Nazi League in 1936, broadcast anti-Nazi news on its local KFWB radio station, and produced *Confessions of a Nazi Spy* (1939), Hollywood's first openly anti-Nazi film, in which my parents' friend, Lotte Andor, appeared. As for Nazi censorship of American films, Hollywood's own Production Code already proscribed negative depictions of other nationalities, nor could sundry local, state, and foreign, non-German-controlled countries' censorship bodies be ignored. Further pressure not to stir the pot, moreover, came from American Jewish organizations, fearful, like the studio bosses, of rising domestic anti-Semitism. But the most resounding rebuttal to Urwand's broadside came in Steven Ross's *Hitler in Los Angeles: How Jews Foiled Nazi Plots Against Hollywood and America* (2017). Even MGM and Paramount, Ross revealed, while placating the Germans on the surface, behind the scenes were helping a Jewish counterespionage ring to thwart a spate of planned terrorist attacks by local American Nazi organizations. These included, as alluded to in Chapter 15, the assassination of Jewish movie people and other bigwigs, the bombing of ports and military installations, and most horrifically, the pumping of cyanide gas, block by block, into the homes of Jewish neighborhoods in Los Angeles.

# appendix j

## ADOLPH ZUKOR AND THE JEWS WHO INVENTED HOLLYWOOD

*Adolph Zukor (1914)*

THE 1989 publication of Neal Gabler's *An Empire of Their Own: How the Jews Invented Hollywood* sent shock waves through much of the Jewish community. Not because the premise was startling, as the disproportionate number of Jews in the upper echelons of the film industry (compared to their tiny percentage of the overall U.S. population) had been an open secret since the 1920s. What was striking, and discomfiting to many, was the brazen manner in which it was expressed. For his critics, Gabler's forthrightness played into the anti-Semites' conspiratorial hands; for many others, whose counterview soon became consensus, it demonstrated a newly emboldened Jewishness that proudly proclaimed Jewish accomplishments rather than shying away from them. An added irony to Jewish uber-influence in Hollywood, as Gabler reminded, was that anti-Semitism itself had propelled it. This extended from the pogroms that had driven mainly Eastern European Jews to the Land of Opportunity in the late eighteenth and early nineteenth centuries, just as the movie industry was emerging. In the United States, the less virulent but still palpable anti-Semitism they confronted, which excluded Jews from more established industries, ironically shunted them into the still fledgling, not yet lucrative, and initially quite disreputable motion picture business. By the time Hollywood became the world's movie capital in the early 1920s, most all the major studios were owned and operated by immigrant or first-generation American Jews: Paramount by Hungarian Adolph Zukor; MGM by Russians Louis B. Mayer and Nicholas Schenck, and Austrian-descended Marcus Loew; Fox (later Twentieth Century Fox) by Hungarian William Fox; Warner Bros. by Polish-born or descended Harry, Jack, Albert, and Sam Warner; Universal by German Carl Laemmle; Columbia by Russian and German-descended Harry Cohn; and United Artists partly by Nicholas's brother, Joseph Schenck. Only First National among the majors was non-Jewish run, and even it would be absorbed into Warner Bros. by the late 1920s. Mega-independent producers Samuel Goldwyn, David Selznick, and Walter Wanger also were Jewish, as were most of the major movie theater owners. Just how insecure Hollywood's Jews remained, despite their enormous influence, was exhibited in their responding to a series of 1920s movie-star scandals by appointing Will Hays, a Protestant deacon and the U.S. Surgeon General, to head a new in-house public relations organization, the Motion Picture Producers and Distributors of America (today the Motion Picture Association of

America, or MPAA). By the time Joe Breen, a well-connected Catholic (and anti-Sem-ite), took the reins of Hollywood's in-house censorship board, the Production Code Administration, in 1934, and with the restructured, Depression-era studios under Wall Street financial control, anyone scratching the surface of purportedly Jewish-run Hollywood would have found the industry beholden to WASP investors, like the Rockefellers, and policed by the Pope.

# appendix k

## GALICIAN JEWS

Galician Jews, 1886

NAMED after a Celtic tribe, the Galics, Galicia was populated in Roman times by a Celto-German tribal admixture of Celts, Vandals, and Goths. During the Great European Migration (circa 300–600 CE), nomadic Slavs and Croats invaded and eventually dominated the region. Geographically sandwiched among what came to be Poland, Hungary, Moldavia, Transylvania, Bessarabia, and Ukraine, Galicia was batted back and forth between various neighboring countries and kingdoms from medieval times until 1772, when it was awarded to Hapsburg Empress Maria-Theresa (whose Austrian Empire became the dual Austro-Hungarian Empire after 1867). Rich in oil and natural gas, Galicia accounted for 90 percent of the empire's oil supply by 1900 and ranked fourth in the world as an oil producer. Also rich agriculturally, as Granach describes in his autobiography, Galicia became Austro-Hungary's largest and most populous and ethnically diverse province. Its population by 1900 consisted of an estimated 45 percent Poles, 43 percent Ukrainians, 11 percent Jews, 1 percent Germans, plus a smattering of other ethnicities. Jews had migrated to Galicia from Germany in the Middle Ages and by the late nineteenth and early twentieth centuries, while still mostly tailors, craftsmen, and bakers, like Granach's family, had more recently risen to prominence in the legal, medical, and cultural fields. Galician-born Jews who went on to extraordinary achievements outside their native land, besides Granach and the previously noted Billy Wilder, Elisabeth Bergner, and Salka Viertel, include: film director Otto Preminger; philosopher Martin Buber; psychiatrist Wilhelm Reich; Nazi hunter Simon Wiesenthal; cosmetics pioneer Helena Rubinstein; Method acting founder Lee Strasberg; writers S.Y. Agnon, Isaac Deutscher, Stanislaw Lem, Henry Roth, and Bruno Schwarz; Nobel Prize-winning scientists Isidor Isaac Rabi, Roald Hoffman, and Georges Charpac; and Sigmund Freud's mother, Amali Freud. After Austria-Hungary's defeat in World War I and Germany's in World War II, Galicia was split up and reapportioned once again, with the northwestern section ping-ponged back to Poland and the southeastern section going to Ukraine, where they currently remain.

# appendix 1

## VARIAN FRY

*Varian Fry (U.S. Holocaust Memorial Museum)*

NEW YORK City-born Varian Fry (1907–1967) worked as an editor and journalist at several progressively oriented magazines, including *The Nation* and *The New Republic,* before joining the North American Committee to Aid Spanish Democracy during the Spanish Civil War (1936–1939). After Germany's invasion of France in 1940, he helped found the Emergency Rescue Committee (ERC), a private American relief organization devoted to rescuing artists and intellectuals who either had sought refuge from Hitler in France, or who already resided there and suddenly found themselves endangered by the Nazi juggernaut. With Eleanor Roosevelt's assistance, the ERC obtained emergency visas for several of the more prominent, at-risk refugees, and in August 1940, after France's capitulation, Fry went to southern France (then governed by the Vichy puppet regime) to direct the ERC's rescue mission. Together with U.S. Vice-Council Harry Bingham Jr., Fry arranged sanctuary for numerous escapees, with Bingham offering his own home as refuge for Lion and Marta Feuchtwanger, in particular. With the support of French resistance fighters, Fry secured an escape route from France to Spain across the Pyrénées, through which, besides the illustrious figures who were Fry's primary focus, close friends of Rudy and Eva (and later of mine as well), Otto and Eva Pfister, also managed to flee to safety. The legion of notables Fry helped save, in addition to the Feuchtwangers, included anthropologist Claude Lévi-Strauss; Nobel Prize-winner in Physiology and Medicine Otto Fritz Meyerhof; filmmaker Max Ophüls; artists Jean Arp, Marc Chagall, Marcel Duchamp, Max Ernst, Jacques Lipschitz, André Masson, and Roberto Matta; and writers Hannah Arendt, André Breton, Arthur Koestler, Siegfried Kracauer, Heinrich (and his wife, Nelly) Mann, and Franz Werfel (and his wife, Alma Mahler-Werfel). Overall, despite little cooperation and outright harassment from the then still officially neutral U.S. State Department, Fry and his associates at the ERC managed to save the lives of more than 2,000, mostly Jewish refugees. Rather than returning to America a decorated hero, however, Fry was expelled from the renamed International Rescue Committee for his vocal criticism of the State Department. A measure of ironic redemption came after the war, when not the American but the French government awarded Fry the Croix de Chevalier de la Legion d'Honneur, France's highest order of merit, in 1967. Posthumous distinctions included the United States Holocaust

Memorial Council's Eisenhower Liberation Medal in 1991, and in 1994 Fry became the first American citizen recognized in Israel as a "Righteous among the Nations," an honor bestowed upon non-Jews who risked their lives to save Jews from the Nazi genocide.

# appendix m

## FRITZ LANG

*Fritz Lang (1960s)*
*(Alamy)*

AMONG the elite émigrés of the so-called New Weimar, no one's Jewish identity was mired in more mystery and confusion than that of renowned Austrian director Fritz Lang (1890–1976). Lang's Christian father had managed to skirt Austria's anti-intermarriage law by declaring himself "without denomination" so that his wife could retain her Jewish affiliation. Rising anti-Semitic and assimilationist pressures, however, coaxed both parents to convert to Catholicism and to raise young Fritz as a Catholic. Yet the façade was a flimsy one, both for unconverted Jews who considered the converts "Jews under the skin" and for the Nazis who officially determined anyone with even a single Jewish grandparent to be Jewish. Propaganda minister Joseph Goebbels apparently bought the subterfuge enough to offer Lang the job of heading the German film industry in 1933 (Hitler had loved his 1927 film *Metropolis*). But when Lang instead fled to France with his Jewish consort, Lily Latté, the jig was up, as would later be confirmed in the 1940 Nazi documentary *Der Ewige Jude* (*The Eternal Jew*), which inserts scenes from Lang's *M* (1931) as an example of "degenerate Jewish art." Now a classic of world cinema and a forerunner of the dark crime cycle of the 1940s and 1950s known as film noir, *M*, about a serial killer of young girls (based on an actual case), was one of several proto-noirs Lang made in an expressionist style during the Weimar period. His first American film, *Fury* (1935), about vigilante justice, clearly resonated with the rise of Nazism and marked the beginning of a spate of American noirs that would lead to Lang's being dubbed the "master of darkness" and "father of film noir." Surviving a brush with McCarthyism in the 1950s and frustrated by Hollywood's conservative tilt, Lang returned briefly to Germany where he directed three films. He was granted a star on the Hollywood Walk of Fame in 1960 and Jean-Luc Godard honored him with a supporting role, as himself, in the French New Wave classic *Contempt* (1963).

# appendix n

## ROBERT RYAN AND CORNEL WILDE

*Robert Ryan in* Odds Against Tomorrow *(1959), Cornel Wilde in* The Perfect Snob *(1941) (both Photofest)*

THE BOXING SKILLS he'd showcased as a college champion at Dartmouth played a major role in the Hollywood career of Robert Ryan (1909–1973). Soon after entering Max Reinhardt's theater workshop in 1937, Ryan landed a part in the boxing film *Golden Gloves* (1940). Several tough-guy, supporting roles followed, but his breakthrough wouldn't come until after World War II, as the anti-Semitic killer in Edward Dmytryk's *Crossfire* (1947), for which he garnered an Oscar nomination for Best Supporting Actor. Consistent top billing followed, often in film noirs as the villain or sinister presence, befitting Ryan's darkly rugged good looks and imposing stature but not his personality or political ideals. A pacifist, he appeared in war films; an anti-McCarthyist, he starred in anti-Communist ones. Among his most memorable roles were in noirs directed by Jewish émigrés Fred Zinnemann, Max Ophüls, and Fritz Lang. Boxing returned from the repressed in *The Set-Up* (1949), in which his over-the-hill pugilist is brutalized for refusing to take a dive. As Ryan himself refused to do, in rejecting the lucre of episodic television—appearing only in anthology dramas, classics on Broadway, and major motion pictures for the remainder of his prolific career.

What boxing was for Ryan, fencing proved to be for Cornel Wilde (1912–1989), who was not, as his Hollywood bio would have it, born in New York City. Rather, as his birth name Kornél Lajos Weisz indicates, he was brought to America by his Hungarian-Jewish parents at age seven. Multi-talented, and dashingly handsome, Wilde qualified in fencing for the 1936 Olympics, which he turned down to appear in a play on Broadway. In 1937 he toured with Tallulah Bankhead in *Anthony and Cleopatra*, illustrated a fencing textbook, wrote a fencing play, and after serving as Laurence Olivier's fencing coach for a 1940 Broadway production of *Romeo and Juliet*, landed a contract with Warner Bros. His Hollywood breakthrough came with a Best Actor nomination for his lead role in the Frédéric Chopin bio-pic *A Song to Remember* (1945). A pretty boy to Ryan's more ominous heavy, Wilde was often cast as the romantic lead or swashbuckling adventurer, though this did not prevent his appearing in several noirs as well. Wilde formed his own production company in the 1950s and occasionally wrote, directed, and starred, such as in *The Naked Prey* (1956), an African adventure film, which, like the Oscar-winning circus spectacular *The Greatest Show on Earth* (1952), showcased Wilde's athletic physique.

# notes

## PROLOGUE

3    **The London stage adaptation of the movie *All About Eve*:** The 2019 adaptation was written and directed by Ivo van Hove and starred Gillian Anderson as Margo Channing (played by Bette Davis in the film) and Lily James as Eve Harrington (played by Anne Baxter). *All About Eve* had been adapted for the stage in 1970, as a Tony Award-winning musical, *Applause,* starring Lauren Bacall as Margo and Penny Fuller as Eve.

4    **while performing on Broadway in 1943:** Margalit Fox, "Mary Orr, 95, an Author Who Inspired 'All About Eve', Is Dead," *The New York Times*, October 6, 2006, https://www.nytimes.com/2006/10/06/obituaries/06orr.html.

4    **(in the already suggestively titled *The Two Mrs. Carrolls*):** The play would be adapted for a like-titled film noir in 1947, with Barbara Stanwyck in Bergner's stage role and co-starring Humphrey Bogart.

5    **"used her lovers as a springboard for her career":** Gad Granach, *Where Is Home? Stories from the Life of a German-Jewish Émigré,* trans. David Edward Lane (Los Angeles: Altra Press, 2009), 32.

5    **Jews who had fled an earlier round:** Neal Gabler, *An Empire of Their Own: How the Jews Invented Hollywood* (New York: Anchor, 1989).

## CHAPTER 2: MASSEUSE TO THE STARS

13    **"nobler than common sense":** Quoted in Herbert S. Lewis, "Introduction," in Alexander Granach. *From the Shtetl to the Stage: The Odyssey of a Wandering Actor* (New Brunswick, N.J.: Transaction Publishers, 2010), xii.

14    **his trademark "*Schrei*":** Ibid.

14    **"immense vitality of Eastern Judaism":** Arnold Bronnen quoted in ibid.

14    **Weimar era nickname, *König der Ostjuden*:** Gad Granach, *Where Is Home?,* 22.

14    **"cult of the Ostjuden":** Steven E. Aschheim, *Brothers and Strangers: The East European Jew in German and German Jewish Consciousness, 1800–1923* (Madison: University of Wisconsin Press, 1982), 191.

15    **co-writer Walter Reisch:** Screenplay credits also include longtime Wilder writing partner Charles Bracket and Sam Behrman. The script was based on an original story by Melchior Lengyel. Salka Viertel "was responsible" for the film's inception and Gottfried Reinhardt wrote an early script (Donna Rifkind, *The Sun and Her Stars: Salka Viertel and Hitler's Refugees in the Golden Age of Hollywood* [New York: Other Press, 2020], 221).

15 **shot "mitt-out" sound:** The more likely original meaning of MOS is "motor only sync" or "motor only shot."

15 **"Berlin papers were filled":** Gad Granach, *Where Is Home?*, 8.

16 **resettle with her in Vienna:** Email to the author from Lois Roberts, former wife of Gerda's brother Fred Weinman, April 29, 2019; also *De Parelduiker* (the pearl diver), Issue 2010/3. Under her married name, Gerda published two books of photographs: *Helene Weigel, Actress: A Book of Photographs*. Text by Bertolt Brecht, photographs by Gerda Goedhart, ed. Wolfgang Pintzka, trans. John Berger and Anna Bostock (1961); and Gerda Goedhart, *Bertolt Brecht Porträts* (Zurich: Verlag die Arche, 1964).

17 **Eva arrived in America:** Certificate Nos. 6179753 and 619756, U.S. Naturalization Record Indexes, 1791–1992.

## CHAPTER 3: *KRISTALLNACHT*

20 **since labeled *Kristallnacht*:** Michael Berenbaum, "Kristallnacht: German History," in *Encyclopedia Britannica*, https://www.britannica.com/event/Kristallnacht.

20 **stopover in Västraby, Sweden:** Hildegard Feidel-Mertz and Andreas Paetz, *Das Jüdische Kinder und Landschulheim Caputh (1931–1938): Ein Verlorenes Paradies* (Bad Heilbrunn, Germany: Verlag Julius Klinkhardt, 2009).

20 **With that he boarded the next plane:** Gad Granach, *Where Is Home?*, 45.

20 **stayed for a while with his friend, Herman Hesse:** Ibid., 44.

21 **renewed relations with Lotte Lieven:** documentary film *Alexander Granach: Da Geht Ein Mensch* (Angelika Wittlich, 2012).

21 **"hardly a model of compassion":** Gad Granach, *Where Is Home?*, 45.

21 **"something of a hero":** Ibid.

21 **met up with . . . Erwin Piscator and Bertolt Brecht:** Ibid., 46.

22 **"improper moral conduct":** Ibid.

22 **would have his famous novel *Jud Süß*:** A philo-Semitic British film version of the novel was directed by Lothar Mendes in 1934, starring Conrad Veidt. The film was titled *Power* in the United States.

22 **good word from Premier Vyacheslav Molotov's Jewish wife:** Ibid.

23 **In New York he met up with his siblings . . . son, Gad, as well, who had emigrated to Palestine . . . he was treading the boards again.:** Ibid., 47, 48, 69, 75.

## CHAPTER 4: WRITING ON THE WALL

25 **"I fell immediately in love":** Vincent Brook, ed., "Edited Conversations with Rudy," edited transcript of interviews with Rudy Brook, held between July 12, 1982, and September 11, 1983.

26 **"When I laughed and said":** Quoted in Eva Brook, "A Childhood Romance— Which Turned Into Marriage," unpublished essay (n.d.), 1.

27 **"was very important to my mother":** Ibid., 3

28　**"When I was nine years old"**: Eva Brook, "My Mother's Death," unpublished essay (n.d.), 1–5, composited with portions from Eva Brook, "My Artistic Mother" and "My Childhood Happiness," unpublished essays (n.d.).

31　**"handstitched, with flowers and shiny ribbons"**: Eva Brook, "My Artistic Mother" 2.

31　**(trade school for women), which she detested**: Eva Brook, letter to Liselotte, December 17, 1978, 1.

32　**she later wrote, and "became closer"**: Eva Brook, "A Childhood Romance," unpublished essay (n.d.), 2.

## CHAPTER 5: A TASTE OF HONEY

33　**Frank Wedekind's pair of "Lulu" plays:** Wedekind divided *Earth Spirit* into the paired plays that included *Pandora's Box* in 1904.

34　**"There is only Louise Brooks!":** Quoted in Steve Silberman, *Culture*, 04.10.98.

## CHAPTER 6: PANDORA'S BOX

37　***"If I should forget thee, O Jerusalem"***: Psalm 37:5.

38　***"Dann kam Hitler!"***: Eva Brook, letter to Liselotte, 2.

39　**was unable to practice law:** Ibid., 1.

39　**turned an obstacle into an opportunity:** Feidel-Mertz and Paetz, *Das Jüdische.*

39　**where Albert Einstein had spent summers with his wife, Elsa:** https://www.einsteinsommerhaus.de. See also Tom Tugend, "Living in Einstein's House," *Jewish Journal*, September 9, 1998, https://jewishjournal.com/old_stories/1097.

40　**joined a short-lived singing troupe:** Eva Brook, "Friendship," December 1984, unpublished essay (n.d.), 1.

40　**the Nazis' *"vergessene"* (forgotten) schools:** Feidel-Mertz and Paetz, *Das Jüdische*, 24.

41　**Hechalutz lived up to its "pioneer" name:** Israel Ritov and Yehuda Slutsky, "He-Halutz," in Michael Berenbaum and Fred Skolnik, ed., *Encyclopaedia Judaica 8*, 2nd ed. (Detroit: Macmillan Reference USA, 2007), 756–761.

41　**would enable Granach's son, Gad, to emigrate to Palestine:** Gad Granach, *Where Is Home?*, 52.

## CHAPTER 7: BRUCH'S LIST, PART 1

43　**"became a high-ranking member of Hechalutz":** Vincent Brook, "Edited Conversations," 6–9.

## CHAPTER 8: BRUCH'S LIST, PART 2

49　**his other activities with Hechalutz hadn't been illegal:** Vincent Brook, "Edited Conversations," 9.

49 **it was under Haavara's guidelines:** "Jewish Virtual Library: A Project of AICE—Encyclopedia Judaica: Haavara," http://www.jewishvirtuallibrary.org/ haavara.

50 **"The tragic thing about some of my efforts":** Vincent Brook, "Edited Conversations," 9.

51 **Kristinehov Internat, the Jewish boarding school:** Hildegard Feidel-Mertz, *Schulen im Exil. Die Verdrängte Pädagogik nach* 1933 (Reinbeck, Germany: rororo/Rowohlt Verlag, 1983).

## CHAPTER 9:
## *ALLES GEHT CAPUTH* (EVERYTHING GOES "KAPUT")

53 **his part in the devilish ruse:** *Prisoner in Paradise*, a 2002 documentary directed by Malcom Clarke and Stuart Sender.

54 **was subjected to a similar, if less lethal, ignominy:** Feidel-Mertz and Paetz, *Das Jüdische*, 58–59.

55 **The Nazis for years had been harassing the school:** Documentary film *En verschollenes Paradies: Das jüdische Kinderheim in Caputh* (1995, Havel-Film Babelsberg, written and directed by Hans-Dieter Rutsch).

55 **Einstein's summer house . . . was confiscated:** https://www.einsteinsommer-haus.de.

55 **Hostile encounters with Hitler Youth:** Tugend, "Living in Einstein's House."

56 **Gestapo-led foreshadowing of the Holocaust:** Feidel-Mertz and Paetz, *Das Jüdische*.

56 **"My father's being Christian":** Peter Meyer, with Vincent Brook, "Tanks a Lot," unpublished memoir, latest revision October 23, 2017.

58 **Tommi . . . recalls only beginning to grasp what it meant:** Phone conversation with the author, November 24, 2019.

## CHAPTER 10: BAGGAGE CLAIM

61 **"Why *that* far away?":** Eva Brook, "The Middle Years ('Born Again')," unpublished essay, May 1, 1982, 1.

61 **"I saw strange things flying":** Ibid.

61 **had been informed during the war:** "*Familie, Landeshauptarchiv Magdeburg, Stadtarchiv Magdeburg.*"

61 **letter tossed by a fellow inmate:** The diary of Ilse's husband, Karl Meyer.

62 **which included that of Gertrud Feiertag:** Feidel-Mertz and Paetz, *Das Jüdische*.

63 **"*wir kamen hier nur mit $10 an*":** Eva Brook, letter to Liselotte, 1.

## CHAPTER 11: THE MEDIUM IS THE MASSAGE

65 **rumor had it, also her lover:** Rifkind, *The Sun and Her Stars*, 119.

65 **"could firstly (what could I not?), play any role":** Quoted in ibid., 232.

66 **Gerda's practice offered:** Eva Brook, letter to Liselotte, 1.

67 **the trump card was his "powerful personality":** Miriam Rocklin quoted in Lewis, "Introduction," xv.

68 **"He was terrific!":** Ibid.

68 **"The earth in East Galicia":** Alexander Granach, *From the Shtetl*, 1.

68 **"crooked baker's legs" (since straightened in an operation):** Ibid., 172, 180.

68 **"brothers and strangers":** Aschheim, *Brothers and Strangers*.

69 **the longstanding gulf between the Ashkenazi (European) cousins:** Ibid. Also see among others, Michael A. Meyer, *The Origins of the Modern Jew: Jewish Identity and European Culture, 1749–1824* (Detroit: Wayne State University Press, 1967, 1984).

70 **"they all looked down on these filthy peasants":** Paraphrase of a quote by Lawrence Weschler, in Vincent Brook, *Driven to Darkness: Jewish Émigré Directors and the Rise of Film Noir* (New Brunswick, N.J.: Rutgers UP, 2009), 4.

70: **"'We went from Adolf Hitler to Adolph Zukor'":** Quoted in Philip K. Scheuer, "Wilder Seeks Films 'with Bite' to Satisfy 'Nation of Hecklers,'" [1950], in Robert Horton, *Billy Wilder: Interviews* (Jackson: University of Mississippi Press, 2001), 17.

## CHAPTER 12: ONE-DOWNSMANSHIP

71 **could even point to a mother who almost died:** Alexander Granach, *From the Shtetl*, 6.

71 **"not enough to eat":** Ibid., 2.

71 **"*Meschane mokim, meschane mazl*":** Ibid., 34.

72 **"everything in the house . . . stank of sulphur":** Ibid., 35.

72 **"'The Jew, the Jew'":** Ibid., 36.

73 **"TYPHUS!":** Ibid., 39.

74 **"we stole and ate and ate and stole":** Ibid., 40.

74 **"villa-like houses . . . in between lived the Jews . . . people were simply suffocated":** Ibid., 40–42.

## CHAPTER 13: RIFFKELE

75 **"rivalry and greed":** Alexander Granach, *From the Shtetl*, 45.

75 **"We loved our haggard and wonderful rabbi-teacher":** Ibid., 48.

76 **"the teachers treated us like little animals":** Ibid., 54.

76 **"Father, the wind!":** Ibid., 60.

76 **"So the family became smaller":** Ibid., 67.

76 **"firm, round curves, snow-white skin:** Ibid., 81.

76 **"fifty-center":** Ibid., 87.

76 **"Because life is hard and merciless":** Ibid., 95.

## CHAPTER 14: FROM MALKA TO LEMBERG

77 **"*jidl'*"**: Alexander Granach, *From the Shtetl*, 105.

78 **"a full-bosomed, wide-hipped woman"**: Ibid., 112.

78 **"Now I was a man"**: Ibid., 116.

79 **"swinging gait"**: Ibid., 120.

79 **"One evening we went to the theater"**: Ibid., 121.

79 **"and no power on earth could keep me"**: Ibid., 125.


## CHAPTER 15: NEW WEIMAR

81 **"always something exciting going on"**: Gad Granach, *Where Is Home?*, 19.

81 **formed in the early 1940s and called *Die Gruppe***: See Ruth E. Wolman, *Crossing Over: An Oral History of Refugees from Hitler's Reich* (New York: Twayne, 1996).

81 **Weimar by the Sea**: Vincent Brook, *Driven*, 80.

82 **Émigré notables besides Granach**: See for example Salka Viertel, *The Kindness of Strangers* (New York: Holt, Reinhardt and Winston, 1969); Gottfried Reinhardt, *The Genius: A Memoir of Max Reinhardt, by His Son Gottfried Reinhardt* (New York: Knopf, 1979); Ehrhard Bahr, *Weimar on the Pacific: German Exile Culture in Los Angeles and the Crisis of Modernity* (Berkeley: University of California Press, 2007); and Rifkind, *The Sun and Her Stars*.

82 **"Alma, tell us"**: The song *Alma* (Tom Lehrer, 1965).

84 **"fell on his knees before him"**: Gad Granach, *Where Is Home?*, 46.

84 **Lion and Marta had fled first to France**: Lion Feuchtwanger, *The Devil in France: My Encounter with Him in the Summer of 1940*, trans. Elizabeth Abbott (New York: Viking, 1941).

85 **this and other domestic fascist groups**: Steven J. Ross, *Hitler in Los Angeles: How Jews Foiled Nazi Plots Against Hollywood and America* (New York: Bloomsbury, 2017).


## CHAPTER 16: TROUBLE IN PARADISE

88 **"He seemed remote, unapproachable"**: Quoted in Vincent Brook, *Driven*, 82. Peter Viertel's numerous written works include the screenplay for Alfred Hitchcock's *Saboteur* (1942) and the novel and adapted screenplay for *White Hunter Black Heart* (1990), starring and directed by Clint Eastwood, about Peter's relationship with John Huston (played by Eastwood) during the filming of *The African Queen* (1951), to which Peter also contributed.

88 **had fared less well with her other clients**: Eva Brook, letter to Liselotte, 1.

89 **a field then dominated...by the Japanese**: After World War II and their release from the camps, the Japanese would return in large numbers to gardening in Los Angeles. By the 1960s and 1970s, however, as the Japanese assimilated, this occupational niche would be filled mainly by immigrant and American Latinos.

90    **"nothing against the Japanese"**: Transposed from the author's conversation with Rudy.

## CHAPTER 17: AULD LANG SYNE

91    **"Fritz Lang drove me crazy"**: Vincent Brook, "Edited Conversations," 16.

92    **Bergner..."the great love of his life"**: Gad Granach, *Where is Home?*, 32.

93    **"the fence bordering the Harold Lloyd estate"**: Vincent Brook, "Edited Conversations," 10.

94    **"'Oh, you refugees!'"**: Ibid., 11.

95    **"My best and most loyal helper was Jack Opels"**: Ibid., 15.

## CHAPTER 18: RHAPSODY IN RED

97    **"When I want to envision how royalty must have lived"**: Vincent Brook, "Edited Conversations," 17.

97    **"'and you know what happened in Germany!'"**: Ibid., 18.

98    **"it was aflame with fall color"**: Ibid., 12.

99    **"Through Robert Ryan's business manager"**: Ibid., 17

99    **"I had never heard of him before"**: Ibid., 13.

100  **"We had started a big landscape job"**: Ibid., 16.

100  **"nobody I know of has ever seen Judy Garland"**: Ibid., 14.

## CHAPTER 19: UNHOLY TRINITY

102  **immersing himself in his work**: The author's casual conversations with Rudy

104  **"I became international in Hollywood"**: Quoted in Lewis, "Introduction," xv.

105  **The Dresdners had found refuge in London**: Eva Brook, "Friendship," 1.

105  **"We had all the right connections"**: Quoted in Wolman, *Crossing Over*, 99.

## CHAPTER 20: DOUBTING THOMAS

107  **"sharing my Tommy with her"**: Eva Brook, "Friendship," 1.

110  **"He could never feel too comfortable"**: Gad Granach, *Where Is Home?*, 1–2.

111  **"your mother is so petit bourgeois"**: Ibid., 6.

## CHAPTER 21: "POP GOES THE WEASEL"

113  **"We were snobbish"**: Quoted in Wolman, *Crossing Over*, 110.

114  **most of them owned by fellow Jewish refugees**: See Michael Meyer, "Refugees from Hitler's Germany: The Creative Elite and Its Middle-Class Audience in Los Angeles in the 1930s and 1940s—Film Noir and Orders of Sunny-Side Up," in *Festschrift zum Geburtstag von Julius H. Schoeps*, ed. Willie Jasper (Hildesheim, Germany: Georg Olms Verlag, 2002), 361.

114  **"But once I discovered this charming little Spanish cottage"**: Eva Brook, "The Middle Years," 1.

114 **"Besides more than a thousand chickens"**: Ibid., 2.

114 **curfew-bound in their homes**: Rifkind, *The Sun and Her Stars*, 299.

115 **Even after Kristallnacht**: Ross, *Hitler in Los Angeles*, 250.

115 **this figure actually rose to 67 percent!**: Steven Carr, *Hollywood and Anti-Semitism: A Cultural History up to World War II* (Cambridge, UK: Cambridge University Press, 2001), 238.

115 **changed their name officially in 1944**: Van Nuys property deed.

115 **"beauty and happiness turned into tragedy and death"**: Eva Brook, "My Artistic Mother," 2.

116 **"His big break on Broadway"**: Gad Granach, *Where Is Home?*, 51.

116 **and a long-distance correspondence thereafter**: Alexander Granach, *"Du Mein Liebes Stück Heimat: Briefe an Lotte Lieven aus dem Exil*, ed. Angelika Wittlich and Hilde Recher (Augsburg: Ölbaum Verlag, 2008).

116 **died of an embolism**: Gad Granach, *Where Is Home?*, 51.

## TIMELINES

127 **1890: Born Jessaya Granach**: Official memorial plaque in Berlin, Germany.

## APPENDIX A: ERNST LUBITSCH AND BILLY WILDER

130 **A comedy star in Germany in the 1910s**: See among others, Scott Eyman, *Ernst Lubitsch: Laughter in Paradise.* (New York: Simon & Schuster, 1993); Herman G. Weinberg, *The Lubitsch Touch: A Critical Study* (New York: Dutton, 1968).

130 **The Galician-born and Vienna-raised Billy Wilder**: See among others, Ed Sikov, *On Sunset Boulevard: The Life and Times of Billy Wilder* (Jackson: University of Mississippi Press, 2017).

## APPENDIX B:
## MAX REINHARDT AND EXPRESSIONIST THEATER

131 **The Austrian-Jewish Max Reinhardt**: See among others, Gottfried Reinhardt, *The Genius.*

131 **worked on an early script (as did she)**: Rifkind, *The Sun and Her Stars*, 221.

131 **Inspired by Post-Impressionist painters such as van Gogh**: See among others, J. L. Styan, "Expressionism and Epic Theatre," in *Modern Drama in Theory and Practice*, vol. 3, (Cambridge, UK: Cambridge University Press, 1981).

## APPENDIX C: HELENE WEIGEL AND ELISABETH BERGNER

133 **The Vienna-born Jewish actress Helene Weigel**: See among others, Jennifer Marston William, "Helene Weigel (1901–1971)," in *The Encyclopedia of Jewish Women: Helene Weigel*, https://jwa.org/encyclopedia/article/weigel-helene. See also Frederic Ewen, *Bertolt Brecht: His Life, His Art and His Times* (New York: Carol Publishing Group 1992).

133 **born in the Ukrainian portion of the province:** See among others, Elfi Pracht-Jörns, "Elisabeth Bergner, 1897–1986," *Jewish Women's Archive Encyclopedia,* https://jwa.org/encyclopedia/article/bergner-elisabeth.

133 **the then already famous actor chose her:** Gad Granach, *Where Is Home?,* 32.

134 **In 1943, while appearing on Broadway in *The Two Mrs. Carrolls*:** Fox, "Mary Orr."

## APPENDIX D: ERWIN PISCATOR AND BERTOLT BRECHT

135 **playwrights and theater producers Erwin Piscator . . . and Bertolt Brecht:** See among others, John Willett, *The Theatre of Erwin Piscator: Half a Century of Politics in the Theatre* (London: Methuen, 1978); Ewen, *Bertolt Brecht;* J. L. Styan, *"Expressionism and Epic Theatre."*

## APPENDIX E: CITY SYMPHONIES

136 **the so-called "city symphony":** Vincent Brook, "To Berlin and Back: City Symphonies," in Vincent Brook, *Truth Be Told: A Comparative History of Documentary Film* (Dubuque, IA: Great River Learning, 2018), Chapter 3.

## APPENDIX F:
## G. W. PABST AND LOUISE BROOKS

137 **Austrian filmmaker Georg Wilhelm (G. W.) Pabst:** See among others, Wolfgang Jacobson, ed. *G. W. Pabst* (Berlin: Argen, 1997).

137 **Kansas-born dancer and actor Louise Brooks:** See among others, Peter Cowie, *Louise Brooks: Lulu Forever* (New York: Rizzoli, 2006).

138 **her informal "blacklisting":** Kenneth Tynan, "The Girl in the Black Helmet," *The New Yorker,* June 11, 1979.

138 **biographer Barry Parris suggests:** Barry Parris, *Louise Brooks: A Biography* (New York, Knopf, 1989), 359.

138 **"There is only Louise Brooks!":** Quoted in Silberman, *Culture.*

## APPENDIX G: HAGANAH

139 **Several small Jewish paramilitary units emerged:** See among others, "The Jewish Defense Organizations: The Haganah," *The Jewish Virtual Library: A Project of AICE,* https://www.jewishvirtuallibrary.org/the-haganah.

## APPENDIX H:
## PERSECUTION OF HOMOSEXUALS IN THE THIRD REICH

141 **Jews were clearly the prime target of the Nazis:** See among others, "Persecution of Homosexuals in the Third Reich," in the *Holocaust Encyclopedia* of the United States Holocaust Memorial Museum, https://encyclopedia.ushmm.org/content/en/article/persecution-of-homosexuals-in-the-third-reich.

## APPENDIX I: HOLLYWOOD AND HITLER

142 **Hollywood's reluctance to confront Hitler:** Ben Urwand, *The Collaboration: Hollywood's Pact with Hitler* (Cambridge, MA: Belknap, 2013); Thomas Doherty, *Hollywood and Hitler: 1933–1939* (New York: Columbia University Press, 2013); Ross, *Hitler in Los Angeles.*

## APPENDIX J: ADOLPH ZUKOR
## AND THE JEWS WHO INVENTED HOLLYWOOD

143 **Neil Gabler's *An Empire of Their Own:*** Gabler, *An Empire of Their Own.* See also Vincent Brook, "Still an Empire of Their Own: How Jews Remain Atop a Reinvented Hollywood," in Michael Renov and Vincent Brook, eds., *From Shtetl to Stardom: Jews and Hollywood* (West Lafayette, IA: Purdue University Press, 2017), 3–22.

## APPENDIX K: GALICIAN JEWS

145 **Named after a Celtic tribe:** See among others, Jonathan Webber, *Rediscovering Traces of Memory: The Jewish Heritage of Polish Galicia* (Bloomington: Indiana University Press, 2009).

## APPENDIX L: VARIAN FRY

146 **New York City-born Varian Fry:** See among others, Sheila Isenberg, *A Hero of Our Own: The Story of Varian Fry* (Bloomington, IA: iUniverse, 2005).

146 **close friends of Rudy and Eva:** Tom, Peter, and Kathy Pfister have co-written an extraordinary history, *Eva & Otto: Resistance, Refugees, and Love in the Time of Hitler* (West Lafayette, IA: Purdue University Press, 2019). The book describes their parents' treacherous escape from the Nazis, their courageous resistance efforts in Germany and France, Eva's involvement with Varian Fry's rescue group, as well as her and Otto's work during World War II with the OSS (Organization of Strategic Services).

## APPENDIX M: FRITZ LANG

148 **Among the elite émigrés of the so-called New Weimar:** See among others, Vincent Brook, *Driven to Darkness: Jewish Émigré Directors and the Rise of Film Noir* (New Brunswick, NJ: Rutgers University Press, 2009).

## APPENDIX N: ROBERT RYAN AND CORNEL WILDE

149 **The boxing skills he'd showcased as a college champion:** See among others, Franklin Jarlett, *Robert Ryan: A Biography and Critical Filmography* (Jefferson, NC: McFarland Classics, 1997).

149 **What boxing was for Ryan:** See among others, Peter B. Flint, "Cornel Wilde, 74, a Performer and Film Producer," *The New York Times*, October 17, 1989.

# index

Academy Awards (Oscars), 3, 5, 6, 130,
    134, 141, 149, 150
*Alexander Granach: Da geht ein Mensch*
    (film, 2012), 120, 121
*All About Eve* (film, 1950; play, 2019),
    2–4, 133, 134, 151
Andor, Lotte, 63, 64, 126, 142
anti-Semitism (Jew hatred), 5, 6, 17, 21,
    23, 39, 72, 73, 104, 114, 115, 142,
    143, 148, 149
Auschwitz, 53, 56, 62, 128, 129
Austria, Austrian, 4, 13, 20, 81, 130,
    131, 134, 137, 143, 145, 148
Austro-Hungarian Empire, 72, 145

Balfour, Sir Arthur (Balfour
    Declaration), 41, 139
Baum, Vicki, 92, 93
Baxter, Anne, 2, 3, 152
*Bell for Adano, A* (play, 1944), 116, 117,
    127
*Bent* (play, 1979), 46, 141
Bergner, Elisabeth, 4, 5, 15, 81, 92, 121,
    133, 134, 145
Berlin, Germany
    Alexander Granach and, 15, 20, 21,
        23, 65, 67, 68, 70, 89, 116, 125,
        127, 133
    Caputh and, x, 39, 128
    East Berlin, 133, 135
    Eva and Rudy Bruch/Brook and, ix,
        x, 27, 29–33, 39, 41, 45, 64, 89,
        128, 129
    Gertrud Feiertag and, 39, 61, 62, 128
    Magdeburg and, 25

Olympic Games of, 54
UFA and, 15
Weimar era and, 32, 130, 131, 136,
    137
West Berlin, 135
*Berlin: Die Sinfonie der Großstadt*
    (*Berlin: Symphony of a Metropolis*,
    film, 1927), 32, 136
Berliner Ensemble, 133, 135
Beverly Hills, ix, x, 93, 94, 98
*Bortsy* (*The Fight*, film, 1936), 22, 127
Brecht, Bertolt, 13, 15, 16, 21, 22, 81, 82,
    103, 133, 135
Bressart, Felix, 8, 15
Broadway (theater district), 3, 4, 92,
    116, 125, 131, 134, 137, 141, 149
Bronnen, Arnolt, 13, 14
Brook, Thomas (Tom, Tommy), 97, 101,
    105, 107–109, 113–117, 119, 120,
    122–124, 128, 129
Brook, Vincent, ix–xi, 100, 116, 120,
    128, 129, 171
Brooks, Louise, 33, 34, 66, 137, 138
Bruch, Elise, 52, 61, 128, 129
Bruch (Brook), Eva Eger
    anxiety about loved ones left
        behind, 61, 62, 115
    Alexander Granach affair, ix, 4, 6,
        16, 65–71, 77, 79, 81, 82, 87, 89,
        92, 101–104, 107–110, 114, 116,
        117, 120, 124, 127–129
    *All About Eve* and, 3
    artist/gymnast as, 31, 32, 66, 122, 129
    chicken farm and, 114, 116, 128, 129
    education, 25–27, 31, 32, 129

émigré/refugee as, ix, 6, 60, 61, 67
father Hans's death, 61, 115, 128,
    129
Fritz Lang and, 87–90
Gerda Weinman and, 16, 52, 63, 65,
    66
Gertrud Feiertag and, 39, 40, 52, 62,
    128, 129
*Gruppe, die* (the Group) and, 81, 113,
    127
Hebrew School and, 25, 26, 128, 129
Holocaust and, 5, 16, 20, 37, 46, 53, 56,
    57, 61–63, 84, 115, 122, 128, 129
*Kristallnacht* and, 19, 55, 63, 101,
    128, 129
Lulu (character) and, 34, 36, 89, 101
Magdeburg and, 25, 27, 28, 37, 128,
    129
marriage/separations, 25, 27, 37, 63,
    128, 129
masseuse as, x, 3, 16, 17, 62, 65–71,
    77, 79, 86, 90, 128, 129
mother Alma's death, 28–31, 129
Nazis and, 4–6, 19, 37–40, 52, 55–57,
    123, 128, 129
New Weimar salons and, 81–90
*Ninotchka* and, 11, 13, 67, 82, 88, 101
*Ostjuden/Westjuden* relationship
    and, 67–70, 108, 110, 111, 124
*Palestine* and, 20, 51, 52, 129
Rudy Bruch (Brook) and, 19, 20, 25,
    26, 32–36, 47, 51, 52, 56, 57, 61,
    90, 94, 100–102, 108, 109, 114,
    119, 122–124, 127–129
shyness/naivité, 3, 20, 34, 122
sister Ilse and, 28–31, 52, 56, 57, 61,
    129
teaching at Jewish school in Caputh,
    x, 39, 40, 52, 55, 58, 128, 129
teaching at Jewish school in Sweden,
    20, 51, 61, 95, 129

teaching at school in Norderney, 38,
    129
teaching kindergarten, 119, 129
Thomas Brook and, 101, 107–110,
    114, 116, 117, 119, 122, 124, 129
Tom Tugend and, ix, x
Vincent Brook and, 100, 119, 124,
    128, 129
World War I and, 28
World War II and, 61, 62, 101, 114,
    115
Bruch, Margot, 26, 52, 61, 128, 129
Bruch, Oscar, 27, 52, 128
Bruch (Brook), Rudy (Rudolf)
    *Agudat Yisrael* (Union of Israel) and,
        43, 44
    Alexander Granach affair and, ix, 4,
        89, 101–104, 107–110, 114, 116,
        117, 120, 124, 127–129
    Amnesty International and, 123, 129
    anxiety about loved ones left
        behind, 61, 62, 115
    arrest by the Nazis, 44–47
    chicken farm/ranch and, ix, x, 97,
        113, 114, 116, 119, 128, 129
    Cornel Wilde and, 99, 119
    Douglas Sirk and, 92, 93
    Elisabeth Bergner and, 4, 92, 133
    Eva Bruch (Brook) and, 19, 20, 25,
        26, 32–36, 47, 51, 52, 56, 57, 61,
        90, 94, 100–102, 108, 109, 114,
        119, 122–124, 128, 129
    émigré/refugee as, ix, 6, 60, 61, 67
    fair housing and, 123, 129
    father Oscar's death, 52, 128
    Fritz Lang and, 87–90
    gardener/landscaper as, ix, x, 5, 58,
        64, 65, 89–103, 119, 123, 128
    Gershwins and, x, 95–99, 113, 128
    Gertrud Feiertag and, 39, 40, 52, 62,
        128

*Gruppe, die* (the Group) and, 81, 113, 127

Harold Lloyd and, 93

Hebrew School and, 25, 26, 128, 129

*Hechalutz* (the Pioneer) and, 41, 43–49, 51, 128

Hildegard Knef and, 92, 93

Holocaust and, 5, 16, 20, 37, 46, 53, 56, 57, 61–63, 84, 115, 122, 128, 129

horticulture classes taken, 51, 64, 98

hyperinflation period and, 27

Jewish Employment Service and, 92, 94

Jewish school in Caputh and, x, 20, 51, 61, 95, 128

Jewish school in Sweden and, 20, 51, 61, 95, 128

Judy Garland and, 99, 100

*Kristallnacht* and, 19, 55, 63, 101, 128, 129

law studies and, ix, 27, 38, 39, 128, 129

Lotte Andor and, 63–64, 128

Lulu and, 34, 36, 89, 101

Magdeburg and, 25, 27, 37, 128

marriage/separations, 25, 37, 63, 128, 129

mother Elise's death, 61, 115, 128, 129

Mrs. Green and, 94

Nazis and, 4–6, 19, 37–40, 42–47, 49, 52, 55–57, 123, 128, 129

New York City and, 62–64, 100, 101

*Ninotchka* and, 92, 101

*Ostjuden/Westjuden* relationship and, 68, 69, 108, 110, 111, 124

Palestine and, 20, 41, 43–52, 97, 112, 128, 129

Peter Lorre and, 91, 92, 119

real estate broker as, 119, 128, 129

Robert Ryan and, 99, 119

sister Margot's death and, 61, 115, 128, 129

Thomas Brook and, 101, 107–110, 114, 116, 117, 119, 128, 129

Tom Tugend and, ix, x

Vicki Baum and, 92, 93

Vincent Brook and, 100, 119, 124, 128, 129

World War II and, 61, 62, 101, 114, 115

Zionism and, ix, 41, 43–51, 64, 105

*Zwanzig Jüdische Sänger, Die* (the Twenty Jewish Singers) and, 40, 105, 128

*Cabinet of Dr. Caligari, The* (film, 1920), 14, 130, 131

Caputh (Jewish school in), x, 39, 40, 52–56, 58, 62, 128, 129

*Casablanca* (film, 1943), 64, 104

Cedars of Lebanon Hospital (Scientology headquarters), 100

Chaplin, Charlie, 7, 16, 82

city symphonies (documentary genre), 32, 136

Cold War, 115, 133

*Confessions of a Nazi Spy* (film, 1939), 64, 104, 142

Czinner, Paul, 133

Davis, Bette, 3, 152

Diessl, Gustav, 34

Dietrich, Marlene, 34, 53, 82, 103, 138

Douglas, Melvyn, 6–9

Dresdner, Richard, 105, 107

Dresdner, Trudy, 92, 105, 107, 108, 115, 116

Eger, Alma Blumenthal, 26, 28–31, 71, 115, 121

Eger, Hans, 30, 31, 51, 52, 57, 61, 128, 129

Eger (Ohře) River, 57

Einstein, Albert, 39, 55

Einstein, Elsa, 39

Elbe River, 24, 25

émigrés (refugees), ix, 4, 14, 19, 26, 65, 68, 84, 85, 92, 94, 95, 101, 105, 107, 111, 115, 141, 146, 148, 149

epic theater, 22, 135

ERC (Emergency Rescue Committee, later International Rescue Committee), 146

Ewige Jude, Der (The Eternal Jew, film, 1940), 73, 147

Expressionism, 14, 131, 132, 137, 148

fair housing, 123, 129

Feiertag, Gertrud, 39, 40, 52, 55, 62, 115, 128, 129

Feuchtwanger, Lion, 22, 23, 69, 82, 85, 115, 120, 127, 129, 146

Feuchtwanger, Marta, 82, 83, 85, 129, 146

film noir, 130, 131, 137, 148, 149

France, 23, 49, 69, 84, 137, 146, 148, 160

Freud, Sigmund (Freudian), 9, 10, 67, 144

freudlose Gasse, Die (Joyless Street, film, 1925), 15, 137

Fry, Varian, 84, 146, 147, 161

Führer schenkt den Juden eine Stadt, Der (The Führer Gives a City to the Jews, film, 1942), 53, 55, 56

Gabler, Neal, 142

Galicia, Austro-Hungarian Empire, 21, 65, 68, 70–79, 110, 127, 130, 133, 145

Garbo, Greta, 7–9, 13, 15, 16, 34, 65, 82, 92, 130, 131, 138

gardening (horticulture, landscaping), x, 5, 51, 58, 64, 65, 89–95, 99–101, 103, 119, 128

Garland, Judy, 99, 100

gays (lesbians, homosexuals, LGBTQs), 40, 45, 46, 141

Gelle Latte, Die (The Yellow Patch, play, 1933) and, 21, 127

Gerron, Kurt, 53–55

Gershwin, George, x, 96

Gershwin, Ira, x, 96, 97, 113, 128

Gershwin, Leonore (Lee), 96–98, 113, 128

Goebbels, Joseph, 19, 88, 148

Gold Rush, The (film, 1925), 7

Granach, Alexander
    A Bell for Adano and, 116, 117, 127
    Alexander Granach: Da geht ein Mensch and, 120, 121
    anti-Semitism and, 6, 17, 72, 73, 114
    autobiography, 68, 78, 145
    Berlin career, 4, 5, 12–17, 20, 127
    Bertolt Brecht and, 13, 21, 22, 81, 82, 103
    Bortsy (The Fight) and, 22, 127
    Bretzele's brothel and, 78, 79
    Broadway (theater district) and, 116, 117, 127
    death, 116, 117, 127
    Elisabeth Bergner and, 4, 5, 15, 81, 92, 121, 133, 134
    Erwin Piscator and, 21, 22
    Eva Bruch (Brook) affair, ix, 4, 6, 16, 65–71, 77, 79, 81, 82, 87, 89, 92, 101–104, 107–110, 114, 116, 117, 120, 124, 127–129
    exile in Poland/USSR, 21–23, 43, 127, 133
    family members and, 23, 71–79, 83, 88, 89, 110, 115
    Faust (play) and, 12
    Feuchtwangers and, 22, 23, 82, 84, 120, 127
    For Whom the Bell Tolls (film, 1943) and, 104

Galician upbringing, 68, 70–79, 110,
127, 133, 145
*Gelle Latte, Die (The Yellow Patch)*
and, 21, 127
*Gruppe, die* (the Group) and, 81, 113,
127
*Halfway to Shanghai* (film, 1942)
and, 104
*Hangmen Also Die!* and, 103, 104,
127
Helene Weigel and, 15, 81
Hermann Hesse and, 20, 21, 81
*Hitler Gang, The* (film, 1944) and,
104
Hollywood career, 4, 7–11, 82, 88,
101, 103, 104, 113, 116, 124, 127
Josef Stalin and, 23, 84, 127
*Kameradschaft (Comradeship)* and,
12, 14, 37, 127, 137
"King of the Eastern Jews," 14, 65,
127
*lasterhafte Herr Tschu, Der (The
Licentious Mr. Chu*, play, 1922)
and, 133
Leopold Jessner and, 23
Lotte Lieven and, 21, 23, 92, 116,
121, 127, 133
Malka (Galician woman) and, 77–78,
127
massage and, 4, 16, 65–68, 71, 77,
79, 86, 88, 129
Max Reinhardt and, 13, 82, 125, 131
*Merchant of Venice, The*, and, 13, 127
Molotovs and, 22, 23
Nazis and, 4–6, 20–23, 68, 84, 103,
104, 127
New Weimar and, 81–89, 120
New York City and, 20, 65, 116, 117,
127
*Ninotchka* and, 6–11, 13, 67, 101, 127
*Nosferatu* and, 12, 14, 125, 127, 132

*Ostjuden/Westjuden* relationship
and, 14, 67–70, 108, 110, 111,
124, 127, 133
*Psoledniy tabor (Gypsies)* and, 22
Rabbi Schimshale and, 75
Riffkele (Galician woman) and,
75–77, 127
Rudy Bruch (Brook) and, ix, 4, 6, 16,
65–71, 77, 79, 81, 82, 87, 92, 101,
102. 107–110, 114, 116, 117, 120,
124, 127–129
Salka Viertel and, 65, 82, 83, 87, 88
*Seventh Cross, The* (film, 1944) and,
127
*So Ends the Night* (film, 1941) in, 104
son Gad Granach and, 5, 16, 20, 21,
23, 41, 81, 88, 89, 92, 110, 111,
116, 127, 133
*Voice in the Wind* (film, 1944) and,
104
wife Martha Guttmann and, 20, 23,
71, 88, 110, 127
womanizer, 4, 15, 16, 66, 67, 81, 86,
88, 89, 92, 121
Granach, Gad, 5, 16, 20, 21, 23, 41, 81,
88, 89, 92, 110, 111, 116, 127, 132
Grauman's Chinese Theater, 101, 102
Great Purge (USSR), 22, 127
*Gruppe, die* (the Group), 81, 113, 127

*Haganah* (the Defense), 44, 45, 49, 141,
142
*Hangmen Also Die!* (film, 1943) and,
103, 104, 127, 133, 135
*Hechalutz* (the Pioneer), 41, 43, 45, 49,
51, 123, 129
Hesse, Hermann, 20, 21, 81
Hindenburg, Paul von, 38
Hitler, Adolf (the Führer), 20, 23, 38, 39,
49, 54, 55, 70, 86, 135, 138, 142, 143,
147, 149

Hitler Youth, x, 55, 56
Hollywood (district in Los Angeles), 17,
    65, 94, 97, 107, 128, 129, 148
Hollywood (movie industry), ix, xi, 3–5,
    7, 10, 15, 16, 23, 25, 63, 64, 69, 70, 82,
    88, 89, 97, 101, 102, 104, 113, 116,
    124, 127–131, 133–135, 137, 138,
    142–144, 148–150
Hollywood Anti-Nazi League, 142
Holocaust, the (Shoah), 5, 16, 20, 37, 46,
    53, 56, 57, 61–63, 84, 115, 122, 128,
    129, 141, 146, 147
House Committee on UnAmerican
    Activities (HUAC), 133, 135
hyperinflation period in Germany,
    27

Ikenberg, Ann ("Annchen"), 105, 106,
    108, 113, 116
Ikenberg, Fred, 105
Ince, Thomas (Inceville), 84
Israel, xi, 41–44, 51, 115, 137, 138, 147
Izbica, Poland, 61

Japanese gardening/landscaping, ix,
    90, 156
Japanese internment, ix, 6, 89, 115, 156
Jews, Jewish
    Adolf Hitler and, 20, 23, 38, 39, 49,
        54, 55, 70, 86, 134, 137, 141, 142,
        146, 148
    Agudat Yisrael (Union of Israel), 43,
        44
    Aliyah (Jewish immigration to
        Palestine/Israel), 51, 128, 129,
        139
    anti-Semitism, 5, 6, 17, 21, 23, 39, 55,
        72, 73, 104, 114, 115, 142, 143,
        148, 149
    Arab-Israeli conflict, 43, 139, 140
    Ashkenazis, 69

Caputh and, x, 39, 40, 52–56, 58, 62,
    128, 129
concentration camps and, 20, 53, 56,
    61, 62, 128, 129
Final Solution and, 49, 61
German Jews, 14, 19, 68
Haavara (transfer) Agreement and,
    48–50
Hachsharah (Preparation) and, 41
Haganah (the Defense) and, 44, 45,
    49, 139, 140
Halutzim (Jewish pioneers) and, 50
Hashomer Hatzair (the Young
    Guard) and, 41
Hechalutz (the Pioneer) and, 41, 43,
    45, 49, 51, 123, 128
Holocaust and, 5, 16, 20, 37, 46, 53,
    56, 57, 61–63, 84, 115, 122, 128,
    129, 141, 146, 147
Israel and, xi, 41, 43, 44, 51, 115,
    138–140, 147
Jewish Employment Service, 92, 94
Jewish boarding schools, x, 20, 39,
    40, 51–56, 58, 62, 128, 129
kibbutz and, 20, 52, 97, 112,
Kindertransport and, 61
Kristallnacht and, 18–21, 23, 37, 55,
    56, 61, 63, 65, 101, 105, 115, 128,
    129
Madagascar Plan and, 49
Nazis and, 4–6, 19–23, 37–40,
    42–47, 49, 52, 55–57, 68, 84, 103,
    104, 123, 127, 141, 146, 147, 160
Neturei Karta (Guardians of the
    City) and, 43, 44
NSDAP (National Socialist German
    Workers Party) and, 39
Nuremberg Laws and, 39, 55
Ostjuden/Westjuden relationship, 14,
    67–70, 108, 110, 111, 124, 127,
    133

Palestine settlement and, ix, 20, 23, 41–44, 49–52, 63, 64, 105, 128, 129
religious practices/references, 35–37, 77, 120
ultra-Orthodox, 42–44, 79
Wannsee Conference and, 49
Zionism and, ix, 40, 41, 43, 44, 49–51, 64, 68, 105
*Jud Süß* (*Süss the Jew*, novel, 1925; film, 1940), 22, 152

*Kameradschaft* (*Comradeship*, film, 1931), 12, 14, 37, 127, 137
Knef, Hildegard, 92, 93
*Kristallnacht* (Crystal Night, Night of the Broken Glass), 18–21, 23, 37, 55, 56, 61, 63, 65, 101, 105, 115, 128, 129

Lamarr, Hedy, 103
Lang, Fritz, 82, 87–92, 101, 104, 132–134, 148, 149
Langlois, Henri, 34, 137
Latté, Lilly, 87, 148
Lehrer, Tom, 82
Lieven, Lotte, 21, 23, 92, 116, 121, 127, 133
London, England, 3, 105, 134
Lorre, Peter, 82, 91, 92, 119
Los Angeles, California, ix, xi, 3, 6, 16, 62, 63, 65, 68, 81, 82, 86, 89, 94, 101, 102, 105, 106, 111, 114, 128, 129, 133, 137, 142
Lubitsch, Ernst, 7, 9, 10, 13, 14, 70, 82, 130, 131
Lulu (character), 33, 34, 36, 89, 101, 137, 138
Lund, Sweden, 56, 57, 126, 127

*M* (film, 1931), 91, 148
Magdeburg, Germany, 24, 25, 27, 28, 37, 56, 86, 129, 129

Mahler, Alma (also Mahler Gropius Werfel), 82–84, 146
Mankiewicz, Joseph, 5
Mann, Heinrich, 81, 82, 84, 146
Mann, Nelly, 82, 84, 146
Mann, Thomas, 81, 82
*Marathon Man* (film, 1973), 64
massage, masseuse, 3, 10, 15, 16, 62, 65–68, 71, 86–88, 90, 128, 129
Marx, Karl (Marxist), 9, 10
Mayer, Helene, 54
Mayer, Louis B., 10, 143
McCarthy era, 10, 58, 148, 149
*Merchant of Venice, The* (play, 1921) and, 13, 127
Meyer, Christian, 54, 58, 59
Meyer, Ilse Eger, 26, 28–31, 51, 52, 54, 56, 58, 61, 128, 129
Meyer, Karl, 51, 52, 54, 56, 128, 129
Meyer, Michael, 54, 58, 59, 103
Meyer, Miriam (née Herschorn), 59, 68
Meyer, Peter, 51, 54, 56–59, 128, 129
Meyer, Tommi, 54, 58, 59
MGM (Metro Goldwyn Mayer) studios, 6, 10, 13, 70, 77, 130, 142, 143
Minnelli, Liza, 100
Minnelli, Vincente, 99, 100
Molotov, Polina, 22, 23
Molotov, Vyacheslav, 22, 23
Murphy Ranch, 85, 86

Nazis and, 4–6, 19–23, 37–40, 42–47, 49, 52, 55–57, 68, 84, 103, 104, 123, 127, 141, 146, 147, 160
New Weimar (Ghetto under Pacific Palms, Weimar by the Sea), 80–82, 85, 86, 120, 147
New York City, 20, 23, 41, 42, 62–65, 81, 90, 101, 105, 116, 117, 128, 129, 134, 135, 145, 148

*Ninotchka* (film, 1939), 6–9, 21, 65, 67, 82, 88, 92, 101, 103, 104, 116, 127, 129, 130, 151

Norderney, Germany, 38, 39, 129

*Nosferatu* (film, 1922) and, 12, 14, 125, 127, 132

Odenheimer, Dorothea (Doro), 58, 118, 119

Odenheimer, Fred, 58, 103, 118, 119

Odenheimer, Michael (Mike), 118, 119

Olivier, Laurence, 64, 133, 149

Olympic Games (1936), 54, 149

Opels, Jack ("Fucka Juckah"), 95, 98

Orr, Mary, 5

*Ostjuden* (Eastern European Jews), 14, 65, 67–70, 108, 110, 111, 124, 127, 133, 141

Owens, Jesse, 54

Pabst, Georg Wilhelm (G. W.), 14, 15, 33, 37, 137

Pacific Palisades, California, x, 80, 82, 84, 129

Palestine, ix, 20, 23, 41–44, 49–52, 63, 64, 105, 128, 129

Palfi, Victor, 63

*Pandora's Box* (*Die Büchse der Pandora*, film, 1929), 33, 34, 37, 66, 89, 137

Paris, France, 7, 130, 136

Pfister, Eva, 145, 160

Pfister, Otto, 145, 160

Piscator, Erwin, 21, 22, 135

Poland (Polish), 4, 6, 21, 43, 49, 61, 68–70, 72, 73, 104, 128, 129, 143, 145

*Prisoner of Paradise* (film, 2002), 54–58

*Psoledniy tabor* (*Gypsies*, film, 1936), 22

Pyrenees mountains, 84, 146, 160

Queen of Angels Hospital (the Dream Center), 101

Red Cross, 54

Reinhardt, Gottfried, 82, 131, 151

Reinhardt, Max, 13, 14, 82, 127, 131, 132

Rochlin, Miriam, 67, 68

Roman, Martin (and his Ghetto Swingers), 53

Romanis, 22, 40, 127, 141

Roosevelt, Eleanor, 145

Ross, Steven, 86, 142

Ruman, Sig, 8, 15

Ruttmann, Walter, 32, 136

Ryan, Robert, 99, 119, 149

salon (social gathering), salonnière, 81, 82, 87, 89, 113, 120, 127

San Fernando Valley, California, ix, 58, 97, 113, 114, 128, 129

Santa Monica Mountains, 84, 87

Scheyer, Galka, 82, 83

Schindler, Oscar, 49

Sherman, Martin, 46, 140

*Siddhartha* (novel, 1922), 21

*Silk Stockings* (play, 1955; film, 1957), 92

Sirk, Douglas, 92, 93

Silver Legion (Silver Shirts), 85, 86

Soviet Union (Soviet, USSR), 7, 9, 21, 23–25, 43, 58, 127, 133, 135, 136

Spanish Flu, 30

Stalin, Josef (Stalinist), 7, 22, 23, 84, 127

*Steppenwolf* (novel, 1927), 21

Streicher, Julius, 104, 127

Theresienstadt (Terezín), 53–57, 59, 61, 128, 129

Tugend, Tom, ix-xi, 5, 39, 55, 139

*Two Mrs. Carrolls, The* (play, 1943; film 1947), 4, 134, 151
UFA (*Universum-Film Aktiengesellschaft*) studios, 15
Ukraine, 21, 78, 145

Van Nuys, California, 113, 116, 119, 121
Västraby, Sweden, 51, 128
VE-Day, 24, 25, 61, 119
Veidt, Conrad, 14, 104, 130
Vienna, Austria, 16, 70, 130, 133
Viertel, Berthold, 13, 82
Viertel, Peter, 88, 157
Viertel, Salka, 82, 83, 87, 88, 115, 131, 145, 151
Villa Aurora, 82, 85, 87, 120, 129

Warner Bros. studios, 130, 142, 143, 149
Wedekind, Frank, 13, 33, 137
Weigel, Helene, 15, 81, 133–135
Weimar era/period, 4, 6, 14, 15, 19, 32, 37, 53, 67, 68, 81, 86, 92, 101, 130, 131, 133–135, 137, 141, 148
Weinman (Goedhart), Gerda, 16, 52, 63, 65, 88, 101, 152
Werfel, Franz, 82, 85, 146
*Westjuden* (Western European Jews, German Jews), 14, 19, 68, 69, 110, 11, 113, 120, 122, 124
Westside (of Los Angeles), 82, 87
Wilde, Cornel, 99, 119, 149, 150
Wilder, Billy, 10, 13, 14, 70, 82, 98, 130, 145
*Wisdom of Eve, The* (short story, play, 1946), 5
Wittlich, Angelika, 120, 121
Wolf, Ernest, 95
World War I, 4, 6, 28, 30, 73, 110, 136, 145
World War II, xi, 6, 16, 41, 62, 68, 84, 89, 101, 111, 115, 139, 141, 145, 149, 160

Wright, Frank Lloyd, 82, 97
Zionism, ix, 40, 41, 43, 44, 49–51, 64, 68, 105
Zukor, Adolph, 70, 143

# about the author

*Vincent Brook and his wife, Karen*
*(Photo: Michael Locke)*

VINCENT BROOK was born and raised in Van Nuys, California, and has lived for the past forty years with his wife Karen in the Silver Lake district of Los Angeles. He has a PhD in film and television from the University of California, Los Angeles (UCLA), and has taught at California State University, Los Angeles (CSULA), the University of Southern California (USC), and most recently at UCLA. He has authored or edited ten books, most dealing with historical subjects from a media and/or Jewish perspective. Among these are: *Something Ain't Kosher Here: The Rise of the "Jewish" Sitcom* (2003); *Driven to Darkness: Jewish Émigré Directors and the Rise of Film Noir* (2009); *Land of Smoke and Mirrors: A Cultural History of Los Angeles* (2013); and *From Shtetl to Stardom: Jews and Hollywood* (2017, co-editor).